The Mortgage Book

Own Your Home

Without It Owning You

Lee Welfel

The Mortgage Book

This publication is designed to provide accurate and authoritative information regarding the subject matter contained within. It should be understood that the author and publisher are not engaged in rendering legal, accounting or other financial service through this medium. The author and publisher shall not be liable for your misuse of this material and shall have neither liability nor responsibility to anyone with respect to any loss or damage caused, or alleged to be caused, directly or indirectly by the information contained in this book. The author and/or publisher do not guarantee that anyone following these strategies, suggestions, tips, ideas or techniques will become successful. If legal advice or other expert assistance is required, the services of a competent professional should be sought.

All rights reserved. No portion of this book may be reproduced mechanically, electronically, or by any other means, including photocopying, without written permission of the author. It is illegal to copy the book, post it to a website, or distribute it by any other means without permission from the author.

To obtain more copies of this book please visit

www.LeeWelfel.com

ISBN-13: 978-1494434656

ISBN-10: 1494434652

Cover Design: Bryan Pistole, Design Matters, LLC   www.PaperbackExpert.com

Editor: Judith K. Howe

Author Photo: Jeremy DeLon

©Copyright 2013   Lee Welfel   All Rights Reserved

www.LeeWelfel.com

The Mortgage Book

What others are saying about *The Mortgage Book*

"This book will challenge every preconceived notion you've had about the topic of mortgages."

> **David Lukas**
> **Founder, Infinite Financial Services**
> **Author of *Whose Future Are You Financing***

"I have been referring business to Lee for years and have been consistently impressed with his expertise and professionalism. What my clients like is that he always looks at the big picture and gives them options, based on what is best for their financial future. This book furthers his objectives of giving clients more information so that they can reach their financial goals. The concepts he outlines in this book make it a must-read prior to submitting an offer on a property. He does an outstanding job explaining the big picture behind financing a home.

I highly recommend this book to anyone looking to purchase real estate. These concepts will help you in all your financial dealings."

> **Karen Moulton**
> **Realtor, The Property Group**

The Mortgage Book

"This book is an essential companion for anyone looking to purchase a home. With clear and insightful examples, it shows how every homebuyer needs to go about obtaining a mortgage on their property. *The Mortgage Book* will be a must read for all of my clients looking to acquire a home."

> **Jean Noell, Realtor**
> **GRI, CRS, E-Pro**
> **Coldwell Banker RPM**

"This book should be taught to every student in high school. Not only does Mr. Welfel help you navigate the choppy waters of financing a home, but he does so in a clear, concise and entertaining way. By using his tips that he's gained from years in the mortgage industry, a potential homeowner could save thousands of dollars — and enjoy a better life.

Before buying a house, read and study this information."

> **Mark Friedman,**
> **Senior Editor, Arkansas Business**

www.LeeWelfel.com

The Mortgage Book

"Lee has done an amazing job of showing how one of life's biggest decisions of home ownership can incorporate good fundamental principles of effective cash flow management and debt reduction using a balanced approach. His knowledge of mortgage planning and commitment to the process is phenomenal! Lee's 6-Step Mortgage Planning Process is easy to understand while exposing concepts we don't see every day. This book is a "must have" for anyone who wants to make wise decisions in mortgage planning and managing cash flow!"

    Deron K. Hamilton, CPA
    Partner – Denman, Hamilton, & Associates,
    CPA PLLC

"With the ups and downs to the housing market in the past decade, a need for reputable mortgage advice has arisen. Lee Welfel has written a book that provides guidance through one of the biggest financial decisions one will make during their life.

Following his steps will remove the unknown and calm the fears associated with purchasing or refinancing a house. Lee's advice contained in *The Mortgage Book* has your financial interests at heart, allowing you to turn your house in to a home."

    Dr. Seth Wilson, D.C.
    North Little Rock, AR

The Mortgage Book

"Finding and understanding the best mortgage for a dream home can be a confusing experience. The first time I bought a house I was completely overwhelmed by the terms, paperwork, and procedures thrown at me; from the house hunt, to the offer process, to the mortgage process!

Lee, as my loan officer, helped me understand the intricacies of this complex process. Now, in *The Mortgage Book*, Lee sums up his wisdom and years of experience in a simple but very effective manner.

The Mortgage Book doesn't just explain mortgages, but the entire process of buying a house. The language is simple, and thorough explanations are given without bogging the reader down in unnecessary details. Modern strategies for financing and closing on a house tell how to uncover unknown assets, enhance credit ratings, and understand lender requirements, timelines, and more.

Other books of course give some of this information, but this title's expansive subjects and approach make it a top recommendation. I congratulate Lee on this great contribution!"

    Dr. Punkaj Gupta, MD
    College of Medicine - University of Arkansas for
    Medical Sciences
    Arkansas Children's Hospital

The Mortgage Book

Acknowledgements

Primarily, I would like to thank my beautiful wife Kelly for standing by me throughout my career. You have been my inspiration and motivation for continuing to improve myself every single day. I am forever grateful for your patience and continued support. Truthfully, my job pales in comparison to the responsibilities you bear each day as you raise our children. Dylan and Hudson are so very lucky to have such a wonderful woman to call their mother.

I am grateful to be blessed with my wonderful parents, Tom and Julie. I am forever thankful that I have had the two of you in my corner, pushing me to be the best man I can be. You are both the epitome of hard-working role models. Thank you for instilling all of your positive virtues in me. The world would be a better place if all parents were of the same caliber as you two.

Lastly, I want to personally thank David Kopittke and Heath Lehman for taking a chance on me years ago. Thank you for providing me with the opportunity to turn my passion into a career.

The Mortgage Book

Table of Contents

Foreword 1

CONGRATULATIONS! 5

*** WARNING *** 6

Dave and Sue: A Cautionary Fable 7

The Fatal Flaw 22

What Constitutes Due Diligence? 25

Advantages of Working with a Local Lender 29

No Experience Required 34

The 6-Step Mortgage Planning Process 38
    1. Establish the Relationship 40
    2. Ask Yourself the Most Important Question 41
        Points 44
        Fixed / ARM 44
    3. Don't 'Settle' for a Government Loan Program 46
        VA Loans 47
        Rural Development Loans 49
        FHA (Federal Housing Administration) Loans 51
        Conventional Loans 53
    4. Decide if 20% Down is Worth It to You 57
        The Down Payment 57
        Mortgage Insurance 59
    5. Set the Loan Term: 15 versus 30 Year Loans 63
    6. Your Interest Rate - Balance Cost and Rate 67

Lee's Mortgage Formula 70

The Mortgage Book

OTHER FACTORS **73**
    Emotional Factors: Is this a House or a Home? 74
    Credit Score 75
    The Best Interest Rate 78

Why Do Rates Change? **84**
    The Stock Market 85
    Economic Factors and Reports 85
    The Federal Reserve versus the Stock Market 86

The Lender's Compensation **88**

Planning to Prepay Your Mortgage **90**

The Effect of Time **92**

The Effect of T-I-M-E **93**

The Equity Factor **94**

Real Estate Contract Negotiations **99**

Pay More for the House **100**

Tax Deductions for Mortgage Interest **103**

Closing Costs: Get the Bank to Pay Them **105**

Debt Consolidation **107**

Points **108**

The Cost of Waiting to Sell **110**

How to Sell Your House without Moving **112**

Don't Let Your Mortgage Hold You Back **115**

The Steps to Obtaining a Mortgage **116**

In Closing **120**

The Mortgage Book

Mortgage Industry Terms 121
Annual Percentage Rate (APR) 121
Adjustable-Rate Mortgage (ARM) 121
Amortization 121
Appraisal 122
Closing Costs 122
Conventional Loan 122
Credit Score 123
Down Payment 123
Down Payment Assistance 123
Equity 123
Escrow Account 124
FHA Loan 124
Fannie Mae 125
Fixed Rate Mortgage 125
Freddie Mac 125
Good Faith Estimate (GFE) 126
Home Equity Indebtedness 126
Home Inspection 126
Homeowner's Insurance 127
Income Verification 127
Mortgage Insurance (PMI) 127
PITI (Principal-Interest-Taxes-Insurance) 128
Points 128
Prepaids 128
Pre-Qualified Buyer 129
Rural Development Loan 129
Seller Financing 129
Taxes (Real Estate) 130
Termite Contract 130
Title Insurance 130
VA Loan 131

Author Biography 132

The Mortgage Book

Foreword

As someone who actively originated mortgages for seven years, I know firsthand the importance of proper mortgage planning. The majority of individuals look at their mortgage as a necessary evil that they must endure in order to get what they want (their "dream home"). A mortgage is much like a drill. Why would you seek out a drill and purchase one? Is it for the sake of having the drill to display on your mantle? No, you purchase a drill to accomplish a very specific task, such as hanging a picture on your wall. Without the drill, you can't hang your beloved painting. Similarly, without a mortgage, home ownership would be out of reach for virtually everyone. Just like a drill, few people seek out a mortgage because they dream about having one. The fact is that people want their "dream home" and the only way to accomplish this is with a mortgage. Your mortgage is the equivalent to that drill. Yes, it will help you get what you want (your dream home) but with the help of this book, you will come to realize, it's so much more than that. Utilized properly, your mortgage is one of the most powerful "financial drills" that you have at your disposal. It will allow you to accomplish a myriad of tasks over your lifetime that you never dreamed were possible. Regrettably, the mortgage industry is seriously lacking mortgage professionals who recognize the importance of prudent mortgage planning.

Managing your assets without managing your largest debt (your mortgage), is like heating and cooling your home with the windows wide open!

Lee's 6-Step Mortgage Planning Process provides the layman a roadmap to harnessing the full potential of your mortgage.

The vast majority of mortgage loan officers today, tragically, have diminished the process of taking out a mortgage to fixating solely on interest rates and fees. Once you read *The Mortgage Book*, you will realize that a great rate on the wrong mortgage strategy can literally cost you tens of thousands of dollars over your lifetime. Is your goal to achieve the lowest interest rate or save the most money?

Over a lifetime, neglecting to treat your mortgage for what it really is (a powerful financial tool) will have negative implications on every area of your financial life.

The Mortgage Book

No matter if you are embarking on the exciting journey of buying your first home, or you've taken out multiple mortgages, The Mortgage Book will benefit readers from every walk of life. Taking out a mortgage is simply too big of a financial transaction to ignore the truths in this book. Doing so will be to your own peril. The consequences of taking out a mortgage without implementing the topics Lee writes about will cost you dearly. Take the time to read this book. Open your mind. Throw out everything you've ever believed about a mortgage. Frankly, much of it isn't true.

I'm grateful Lee has put in the blood, sweat, tears and hard work to make this book a reality. This book contains real world concepts that you won't learn in school. Ironically in many ways, the practical wisdom that Lee has shared with us is far more valuable than much of what you learned in school. Reading and applying the principles in this book can significantly change your financial outcome.

This book will challenge every preconceived notion you've had about the topic of mortgages. After reading this book, you will no longer look at your mortgage as a necessary evil, but in fact, you will come to realize that with the knowledge you have gained, you are empowered to transform your entire financial future. If what you thought to be true about mortgages turned out not to be, when would you want to know?

Study this book carefully, implement the wisdom contained in these pages and it will forever change the way you look at your financial future.

David Lukas
Founder of Infinite Financial Services
Author of *Whose Future Are You Financing?*
Host of *The David Lukas Show*

CONGRATULATIONS!

If you're reading this book, you're probably about to embark on the great American Dream of home ownership! As wonderful as this dream can be, for some it has turned into their greatest nightmare. Too many people rush into home ownership without considering all the financial aspects, and/or without a thorough understanding of the mortgage planning process. They also fail to ask themselves the most important question that can quickly turn their dream into a nightmare. I'll discuss that question later, in "The 6-Step Mortgage Planning Process."

My desire is to give you the proper perspective on choosing a mortgage, to equip you with the necessary knowledge about home mortgages and to provide you with a proven process for making the best financial decision possible.

*** WARNING ***

You are about to make one of the largest financial decisions of your life. PROCEED WITH CAUTION!

Selecting a mortgage is a decision with many ramifications for your financial future. Whatever you do, don't make the mistake of simply shopping for the lowest interest rate. Instead, search for the mortgage to fit your financial situation, now and in the future.

Throughout this book, my desire is to not only help you learn the right questions to ask a potential lender and yourself, but to also understand how choosing the wrong mortgage can impact your family and your financial future.

Let's begin with a story that illustrates my point...

Dave and Sue: A Cautionary Fable

Let me introduce you to Determined Dave and Savvy Sue, two unrelated individuals, each embarking on their first home purchase. Each earns $75,000 a year; has $50,000 in savings and is buying a $250,000 house.

Both Dave and Sue finalize real estate contracts for the purchase of their new homes on Thursday morning. Their next step in the home-buying process is to secure financing for their mortgage loans. On Thursday afternoon, each begins calling different lending institutions to obtain interest rate quotes for a mortgage on their respective new homes.

Sue calls a local bank and asks for their interest rate on a 15-year mortgage loan. The loan officer's response is not exactly what she expected:

"Why do you want to take out a 15-year mortgage?"

Sue responds, "So I can pay my house off faster. I know you get a lower interest rate on a 15-year compared to a 30-year."

The loan officer concedes that you do indeed get a lower interest rate on the 15-year, but proceeds to spend the next 30 minutes on the phone with Sue, educating her on the different options associated with mortgage loans.

The loan officer explains the mortgage planning process and the importance of integrating her mortgage into her overall financial plan, both short- and long-term. Even though Sue does *qualify* for a 15-year mortgage, it will put her monthly payment out of her comfort zone. Sue would also like to go back to school to obtain a master's degree within the next year or two, and there will certainly be some expenses associated with that goal. Initially, Sue was not factoring this upcoming expense into this financial decision; but now she's wondering how exactly she'll pay for classes.

By the end of the conversation, Sue has begun to understand that there's more to getting a mortgage than just obtaining the lowest interest rate, therefore she decides to get a 30-year mortgage. The 30-year mortgage will fit her specific situation much better than a 15-year.

The loan officer informs Sue that a Jobs Report is due out the following morning, and advises her to lock in her interest rate right away. He tells Sue how economic data like the Jobs Report can swing interest rates very quickly. Sue agrees, and takes off work that afternoon so she can meet with her loan officer to lock in her rate. After her loan officer presents multiple ways to structure her loan, Sue locks in her interest rate and secures a 30-year mortgage at 5%.

On the same Thursday afternoon, Dave also begins calling lending institutions to shop around for interest rates on his mortgage loan. He obtains an interest rate quote of 4.25% on a 15-year mortgage from the first loan officer with whom he speaks. Determined to get the best deal available on his mortgage loan, Dave then calls six other loan officers at six different lending institutions. They all quote a 4.25% rate on a 15-year mortgage. Even the online mortgage company Dave saw advertising a 2.99% interest rate is actually at 4.25%.

"That rate is only for people purchasing a home above $450,000 with a credit score of 820 or higher," states the loan officer from ABC ONLINE MORTGAGES. "Let me speak with my manager to see if we're able to do better. I will call you back before the end of the day, sir."

The Mortgage Book

Dave continues his quest, calling the same loan officer that Sue is working with and gets the same reply:

"Why do you want to take out a 15-year loan?"

Dave's reaction is a little bit different from Sue's. He's not interested in answering questions and he is getting frustrated because he's been on the phone for the past three hours calling different lending institutions.

"Can you beat 4.25% or not?" responds Dave.

"No, sir, I can't," states the loan officer.

Dave immediately hangs up. Thursday afternoon turns into Thursday evening, and he is still waiting to hear back if the manager at ABC ONLINE MORTGAGES can beat the 4.25% rate.

The next morning, Dave comes into work and has a voicemail from the loan officer.

"Mr. Dave, this is Joe from ABC ONLINE MORTGAGES. I have some good news. I've spoken with my manager, and if you can provide that interest rate quote you referenced yesterday *in writing*, we will beat it."

The Mortgage Book

Dave gets excited. He has done his due diligence by shopping around for the lowest mortgage rate, and it's going to pay off. He immediately calls the first lender he spoke with on Thursday and gets the loan officer back on the phone.

"Well, Dave, rates have actually taken a turn for the worse. We're actually looking at 4.625% on a 15-year mortgage today," says the loan officer.

"What?!" yells Dave. "You were at 4.25% yesterday afternoon!"

Calling back the other loan officers he spoke with yesterday yields the same story about higher rates. Dave gets frustrated, hangs up, and calls back the loan officer from ABC ONLINE MORTGAGES.

"Well, Dave, we were thinking that's what had happened. Interest rates have ticked upward. A better than expected Jobs Report was released earlier this morning. Our rate today is 4.5% on a 15-year mortgage."

Dave ends up locking in his 15-year mortgage with ABC ONLINE MORTGAGES at 4.5% (instead of 4.25%)

despite spending numerous hours shopping around to ensure the best interest rate available.

Dave's problems are only beginning. Although Sue and Dave are both scheduled to close on the purchase of their new home in thirty days, they have very different experiences. Everything goes smoothly with Sue; she actually closes on her home a week before the real estate contract's closing date. On the other hand, Dave is having difficulties. For one thing, his loan officer seems to lose everything Dave faxes to him.

"Hey, Dave, it's Joe again from ABC ONLINE MORTGAGES. Do you think you could resend that pay stub from last month?"

Dave continues to comply, and is assured by Joe that there is nothing to worry about regarding his anticipated closing date. Joe assures Dave that they're "pretty much ready to close."

Everything finally seems to be running smoothly, and Dave is set to close tomorrow on his new house when he gets the call.

The Mortgage Book

"Hey, Dave, it's Joe again. I just wanted to let you know we're having some major weather issues up here. We've lost power, and I don't think we're going to be able to get your closing documents out for you to close tomorrow."

"What do you mean, weather issues?" responds Dave.

"Well Dave, our home office is in River Falls, Minnesota. We got 20-plus inches of snow last night. I'm actually calling you from my house. It doesn't look like anyone is going to be able to make it into the office for quite a while."

"Minnesota!!!" exclaims Dave. "Your website has a picture of downtown New York City on it. I thought you were in New York!"

"Oh no, Dave," says Joe. "That's just for looks."

Ultimately, Dave's closing was delayed a week and a half. The delay costs Dave thousands of dollars in rent, storage and additional time he had to take off work.

Obviously, Sue had a much better experience. Moreover, after closing, she continues to reap the benefits of mortgage planning, versus rate shopping. She weighed all her options, and took out a 30-year mortgage at 5%. For Sue, that was the best fit for her short- and long-term financial plan. She had expected to make a 20% down payment to avoid monthly mortgage insurance; however, her loan officer explained that wasn't necessary. Consequently, Sue only used $12,500 of her $50,000 in savings. This resulted in an initial mortgage balance of $237,500. Furthermore, avoiding monthly mortgage insurance kept her monthly payment down.

Following the counsel of her loan officer, Sue decided to make no additional principal payments on her mortgage loan. Dave takes a different approach.

Dave is determined, and wants to get rid of his mortgage as quickly as he can. He fears that if he has a mortgage, he might one day lose his house. He doesn't quite understand how that could happen, but his father says that mortgages are bad, and Dave believes him. So Dave chooses the smallest possible mortgage. He uses his entire savings ($50,000) for his down payment. As a result, Dave only borrows $200,000 compared to Sue's $237,500.

The Mortgage Book

Dave also gets a 15-year loan instead of a 30-year loan. He hates mortgages, and he figures the 15-year loan will get rid of his loan in half the time. Dave also knows this clever ploy garners him a lower interest rate, because lenders charge less interest for a 15-year mortgage versus a 30-year mortgage. While Sue is paying 5%, Dave is paying only 4.5%.

Dave is so obsessed with getting rid of his mortgage that he sends an extra $100 to his lender every month. He knows the more he sends in, the faster he'll pay off his loan. Compared to Sue, Dave has a smaller mortgage, a shorter mortgage, a lower interest rate — and he's adding money to each payment with the noble goal of paying off his mortgage early. Let's compare their monthly payment breakdowns as we look at the chart on the next page.

	Sue	Dave
Monthly Payment (P&I)	$1,275	$1,530
Interest Portion	78%	50%
Tax Savings	$247	$188
After-Tax Payment	$1,028	$1,342

Sue's monthly payment is $1,275. Thanks to amortization, almost all of Sue's payment — 78% of it—is comprised of interest. (See "Mortgage Industry Terms" for an explanation of amortization.) Thus, on an after-tax basis (assuming she's in the 25% federal income tax bracket), Sue's payment costs her $1,028 a month. She's saving $247 a month on her mortgage payments, based on the deduction she's able to take for mortgage interest.

The shorter the term, the more principal you must pay each month; and principal payments are <u>not</u> tax-deductible (only the interest is deductible).

The Mortgage Book

Meanwhile, Dave's payment is $1,530 a month, but only 50 percent is interest. That's because Dave's loan is for 15 years. Even though Dave is paying more per month than Sue is, he's deducting less. Dave's after-tax cost, therefore, is $1,342, significantly higher than Sue's effective payment of $1,028 per month.

Consequently, Sue is paying $314 less per month than Dave is. However, Dave doesn't mind the extra monthly cost, because he knows he'll get rid of his mortgage faster. For the next five years, Sue makes her monthly mortgage payments. Instead of sending an extra $100 every month to her lender, as Dave does, Sue puts that $100 into an investment account. She also chooses to invest the $314 she is saving each month (compared to Dave's payment) into an investment account.

Unfortunately, five years after they secured their mortgages, catastrophe strikes. Dave and Sue are each blindsided by an unanticipated event. Suddenly they both lose their jobs, along with their ability to make their mortgage payments.

Let's determine what shape each is in now to weather this financial storm. Let's recap the decisions Dave and Sue made during the mortgage selection process.

Sue chose to follow the mortgage *planning* process and secured a 30-year mortgage that fit her short- and long-term financial needs. She put down less money and wisely invested the difference.

Dave, on the other hand, wanted to accelerate his mortgage and pay it off as quickly as possible. His only advice came from his father—not a financial professional. He used his entire savings to make a large down payment, chose a 15-year mortgage and made extra payments each month.

Dave's been successfully paying down his mortgage; the outstanding balance is only $140,000. But does that matter? Even without a job, <u>he still has to make his monthly mortgage payment</u>. So, it doesn't matter that his mortgage balance is only $140,000; what matters is that his mortgage payment of $1,530 is due at the end of the month.

This is a real problem for Dave, because with no job, he has no income. He also has no savings, because he's put every available dollar into paying off his mortgage early.

Determined Dave's nightmare is coming true: He's about to lose his house!

Sue, on the other hand, is in a significantly better financial situation. Of course, her mortgage balance is higher than Dave's — $218,000 — but does that matter? What's important is for her to make her $1,275 mortgage payment at the end of the month.

Sue is not in the same predicament as Dave because she has ample savings from her investments (see the chart on next page). Since, she gave the bank a smaller down payment; she was able to invest $37,500. In addition, she took advantage of the fact that her after-tax monthly payment was $314 less than Dave's was. She invested that money as well. Instead of sending $100 a month to her lender as Dave did, Sue added $100 to her investments every month.

The results of Sue's savvy financial plan:

FOR FIVE YEARS, SUE INVESTED:

$37,500 she did not use as Down Payment	@ 6%	$ 50,582
After-Tax Savings from Monthly Payment $314/mo		$ 22,311
Extra $100/Month		$ 6,977
Total Saved after 5 years		$ 79,890

All told, Savvy Sue has $79,890 saved; yet she began with precisely the same situation as Dave. Even though Sue is out of work, **she'll be able to make her mortgage payments for at least another five years**!

How ironic it is that Dave, who wanted to eliminate his mortgage so he wouldn't lose his house, is about to suffer the fate he was so desperately trying to avoid. He has no available savings, and—since he's unemployed—he can't qualify for a loan. All the money he has in home equity is out of reach, since he can't qualify for a new loan with no income.

DAVE'S SITUATION:

Home Value	$ 250,000
Mortgage Balance	$ 140,000
Home Equity	$ 110,000

This fable shows you why it is so important to minimize both your down payment and your monthly payment. By doing so, *you* retain more of your money.

By keeping control of and access to your money, you maintain liquidity. When you give your money to your lender, you lose control of it. After giving money to your lender, the only way to get your money back in a financial crisis is to sell the house—and that's the one thing you don't want to do. You could try to take out another loan against your home to borrow the equity you have built up (refinance), but who in their right mind is going to give you a loan when you have no income to pay it back?

You must remember:

A mortgage is a loan against your <u>income</u>, not your home. The house is simply collateral.

The Fatal Flaw

This example reveals the fatal flaw in the logic of those who lead you to believe paying off your mortgage as quickly as possible is always the best thing to do. Without a doubt, owning a home mortgage-free is an appealing concept; but many times, it is completely unrealistic! Certainly, paying off your mortgage is great—if that's the only thing you need to do with your money. But what about paying for college? Saving for retirement? Caring for elderly parents, paying for car repairs or simply saving for a rainy day (maybe when your income evaporates through job loss or other disaster)?

Indeed, the fatal flaw of those who tell you to do everything you can to pay off your loan as quickly as possible is this:

The Mortgage Book

They are completely ignorant to everything else that's happening in your life—your specific circumstances.

If you succeed in paying off your mortgage, you may fail to pay for college, or cover costs should you lose your job, experience medical problems, marital issues, or have other unforseen difficulties.

That is why you must *not* listen to anyone pretending that paying off a mortgage is the only thing that matters in your financial life. Your life is more complicated than that, and by realizing this, you'll understand how trying to pay off your mortgage, like Dave, can actually be hazardous.

The smarter and safer approach is to acquire a larger mortgage over an extended time so that you retain control of your money. Don't go outside your comfort zone in your quest to be mortgage-free. Minimize your down payment and your monthly payment to retain control of as much of your money as possible.

Americans devote the largest portion of their incomes to housing; consequently, how you handle the financing of your home will have far-reaching implications on virtually every facet of your financial life. This includes your ability to save, pay for college and plan for your retirement. The mortgage-planning process is about integrating your mortgage into your overall long- and short-term financial goals. Your mortgage is one of the most powerful financial tools at your disposal. The ways in which you handle your equity and manage your mortgage are extremely crucial.

It's evident that Sue recognized she was working with someone who understood these concepts and cared about her overall financial picture. The type of mortgage she took out put her in a better overall financial position than if she'd chosen the lowest rate option. Unfortunately, the mortgage industry is inundated with people who don't consider their clients' overall financial picture.

Do not entrust this process to someone who has reduced such an important transaction in your life to merely rates and fees. Unfortunately, many loan officers have commoditized the mortgage industry by trying to make it *only* about the lowest rate (like shopping for a can of peas at the store). They have become nothing more than order takers.

The Mortgage Book

The way you structure your mortgage is far more crucial to your financial future than any other aspect of your mortgage.

Yes, the interest rate and fees you pay on a mortgage are important, but overlooking all other aspects of your financial life can cost you dearly. Utilized properly, your mortgage can play an integral part in reaching your short and long-term financial goals, thus securing your future.

What Constitutes Due Diligence?

For the average American, your mortgage is your largest debt. Consequently, obtaining a mortgage is one of the largest financial decisions of your life. It should not be taken lightly, or treated as a lowest-cost decision. Since your mortgage plan influences every other facet of your financial health, you must exercise due diligence by working with a seasoned and reputable mortgage lender who:

- understands the market
- uses a defined mortgage planning process

- has the knowledge to close your loan on time (as promised); and
- most importantly, seeks to excel at client services, including considering all factors related to the client's entire financial picture

Unfortunately, Dave didn't take any of this into consideration when obtaining his mortgage. He *thought* he knew what was best and that shopping for the best interest rate constituted due diligence. He dismissed the thought of using a mortgage planning process to integrate his mortgage into his overall financial picture. It's evident Dave's decision led to the realization that his dream had turned into a nightmare.

Most homebuyers expect to get the best possible interest rate on their home loan. That's understandable, but it's *not* the most important part of securing a mortgage. I speak with multiple homebuyers on a daily basis; frequently, I get the feeling many of them view lenders as the enemy. Unfortunately, some lenders should be regarded with caution and avoided at all costs.

That's why you must perform <u>your due diligence</u>.

When shopping for a lender to secure financing on your home, the key is not to fixate your attention on components like rates and fees, but to actually interview lenders on their philosophies regarding mortgage *planning*. Everyone's situation is different. It will be in your best interest to find a lender who recognizes this and is willing to work with you to design a plan that specifically meets your needs. Unfortunately, those homebuyers who think they already know what's best for them let their egos (or fear) hinder their ability to obtain and implement good financial advice.

Looking back at Dave and Sue, who do you think did a better job in solidifying their mortgage loan? Dave spent hours upon hours calling many different lenders, shopping around for the "best" interest rate available on his loan. Eventually, Dave locked in his interest rate with the lender who was able to provide the best rate on that specific day. Sue only talked to one lender, and, based on her trust of his expertise, immediately locked in her mortgage loan.

Very often, the loan officer quoting the lowest possible rate over the phone does not have a mortgage *planning process* in place to meet the homebuyer's needs. Many items other than rates and fees need to be considered when working through the mortgage planning process, including:

- tax deductibility
- down-payment options
- the different mortgage loan programs available
- principal prepayment
- overall financial planning.

You will see very quickly that someone who puts together a comprehensive mortgage plan brings significantly more to the process than someone who simply sees your mortgage as a commodity attached to an interest rate. Make sure *your* loan officer takes the time to educate you in other areas of your financial life, as well as your mortgage loan. This type of professional will help you to save money and, often, to increase your overall net worth.

It's worth investing your time to seek out a professional who has your best interest in mind. Unlike Dave, Sue put her ego aside and let herself be educated on the mortgage planning process. At the end of the story, I think we can all agree that Sue, not Dave, was the one who did her due diligence correctly and secured the financing and mortgage plan that best suited her needs.

Advantages of Working with a Local Lender

As I've said before, a mortgage is probably the largest debt you'll ever assume, and it must be taken very seriously. It's not like shopping for the best interest rate on a credit card. Although the Internet is a great asset in many areas of life, it does have limitations and downsides. Dave learned this the hard way.

When Dave's closing day arrived, a snowstorm stopped the entire process and ended up causing Dave considerable stress, frustration and money. Sue, on the other hand, worked with a local lender who knew the market. His experience and prior relationships with local title companies, insurance agents and appraisers all allowed him to close Sue's transaction ahead of schedule.

The Internet is wonderful and many of us use it every day. It's great for doing research and making routine purchases, but it is not good for making complex purchases or for something as crucial to your future as obtaining a mortgage.

Today, in the mortgage industry, there really is no such thing as a simple "rate quote". Interest rates and closing costs should be completely customized to each homebuyer's property and borrowing situation. The variety of factors contributing to an interest rate requires the lender to completely understand a person's financial picture before giving an accurate loan quote.

I like to use this analogy:

Asking someone for an interest rate quote without completing a loan application, providing all the proper documentation, and actually meeting with that loan officer to discuss the specifics involved with your situation is like asking your doctor for a diagnosis and a prescription without ever getting a physical check-up, having tests or giving a medical history.

It is considered negligence.

Now you may be thinking – hey, I'm a smart-enough person – how could I be misinformed during this process? And who would want to fool me?

Excellent questions – here are some answers.

1. *Unethical lenders may try to take advantage of your understandable stress while you're in this process.* Since buying or refinancing a home is one of the

largest financial decisions you will ever make, you are bound to experience some throughout the process. Unethical providers, out to make a quick buck, who do not have your best interest at heart, may try to take advantage of you. For example, they may tell you to "quickly come into the office and get all the paperwork signed, rates are changing". Not true – an ethical lender will never make you feel panicked or pressured about making a financial decision of this magnitude. Furthermore, once you are truly ready, a rate can be locked-in easily right over the phone.

2. *Unscrupulous lenders will also promote "free appraisals" or "discounted origination fees".* This sounds great, but be aware these charges will appear somewhere. Interest rates and closing costs go hand in hand, so it is important to review the overall loan package, not just individual items that seem discounted. All lenders work with the same financial markets with essentially the same profit margins. Do lenders make money on your loan? Certainly, just as you get paid for working at your job. What a reputable lender seeks for you is the best balance between a great interest rate,

reasonable closing costs and the best fit for your financial situation and goals.

3. *Newspaper or online advertisements are rampant with misinformation, designed solely to get the phones ringing.*

Rates change so quickly that, by virtue of being in print or on the radio, they are almost certain to be outdated. The trick is, lenders can say or print anything – their only purpose is to make their phones ring. When you call referencing the advertised rate the lender responds with "Well, it's wonderful that you called! Rates did go up a bit this morning, but let's talk a little more about you…." A-a-a-and, they're off to the races! A local lender with real-time access to rates won't entice you with gimmicks.

4. *Internet mortgage companies are not regulated.* Online lending is particularly scary because anyone can set up a mortgage website; the person behind that great online rate could be some guy working out of his basement (in Florida) who just started in the business. The danger here, to use just one example, is that closing costs vary significantly

from state to state, and out-of-state lenders, unaware of local and state requirements, frequently misquote fees. I have personally bailed out several people who were lured by a "too good to be true" offer and then the lender failed to come through at the closing. Despite my mortgage banking experience, I would not entrust my own loan to an online, unknown lender. As someone outside the mortgage business, are you really willing to assume this type of a risk? Be certain you consider all of the costs–including the financial and emotional aspects.

The Internet is geared towards piquing interest. Online lenders don't have existing relationships, and don't work by referral. The perception that you can get better rates from an Internet mortgage company is highly misguided, and Internet companies typically take longer to close your loan than local mortgage companies do. Instead of building this industry and their business through repeat purchases from lifetime customers, Internet-based companies commoditize the industry; they look at your mortgage strictly as a commission and go off seeking the next transaction even before yours is complete.

In Dave's story, his decision to go with an Internet company cost him dearly throughout the process. From the faxes that were "accidently" trashed and emails "accidentally" deleted; these perils are much more likely to occur with an Internet company than when you're working with someone who's right down the street, whom you can look in the eyes. In today's environment, it is extremely important that you work with a dedicated and experienced local professional who can navigate you through the mortgage planning process.

No Experience Required

I'd like to close by sharing some information about mortgage loan originators. Not many people know this, but there is actually no experience required to become a mortgage loan originator. Furthermore, before the SAFE Act* passed in 2008, mortgage loan originators needed no license, no special certification, and were not required to complete any continuing education courses. If you could sit in a chair and talk, you could originate mortgage loans.

The SAFE Act improved regulation of mortgage originators, but I still don't think it's done enough. The

The Mortgage Book

Act requires loan originators to submit to education, testing and background checks to ensure they're suitable for providing the service of originating mortgage loans. The Nationwide Mortgage Licensing System (NMLS) monitors those requirements and provides NMLS ID numbers to qualified originators.

Unfortunately, nationally chartered banks are essentially grandfathered into the system; therefore, their loan officers aren't required to prove their suitability. This is because they are required to complete continuing education that meets the Fed's requirements. Nationally chartered bank employees do not have to pass a test or complete any *mortgage-specific* continuing education courses to keep their NMLS identification number current.

This is unacceptable. Managing your mortgage is just as essential to your overall financial future as managing your assets. So why not police mortgage lenders with the same rigor as financial advisors?

Financial advisors must acquire licensing, certifications and designations for virtually all facets of their business. They as do others within the world of finance must also keep active E&O (Errors and Omissions) insurance to protect companies and individuals against client claims for inadequate work or negligent actions.

Mortgage loan originators are not required to carry E&O insurance. Why is that? A negligent mortgage lender may put a client into a loan costing them an extra $25,000 over the next ten years. Is that not considered negligent work? Since properly managing your debt is just as important as properly managing your assets, why do we not hold the professionals we entrust with both of these responsibilities to the same standard?

I've personally seen mortgage loan originators, hired simply to "fill a seat," who have absolutely no business advising clients on any mortgage transaction. One of the main reasons for this book is to ensure you don't entrust the structuring of your mortgage to an unqualified loan originator. Before selecting a mortgage loan originator, I recommend you ask for *letters of reference* from loans they have closed *in the past few months*. A mortgage loan originator who cannot provide these probably doesn't have recent satisfied clients. If they can't provide references, why would you give them the privilege of doing business with you?

The Mortgage Book

You want to select a mortgage loan originator who has satisfied customers and looks beyond your credit score to ensure your mortgage fits into your financial goals. You want someone who knows and follows the *mortgage planning process*.

*For more information on SAFE, go to:
http://mortgage.nationwidelicensingsystem.org/safe/Pages/default.aspx

The 6-Step Mortgage Planning Process

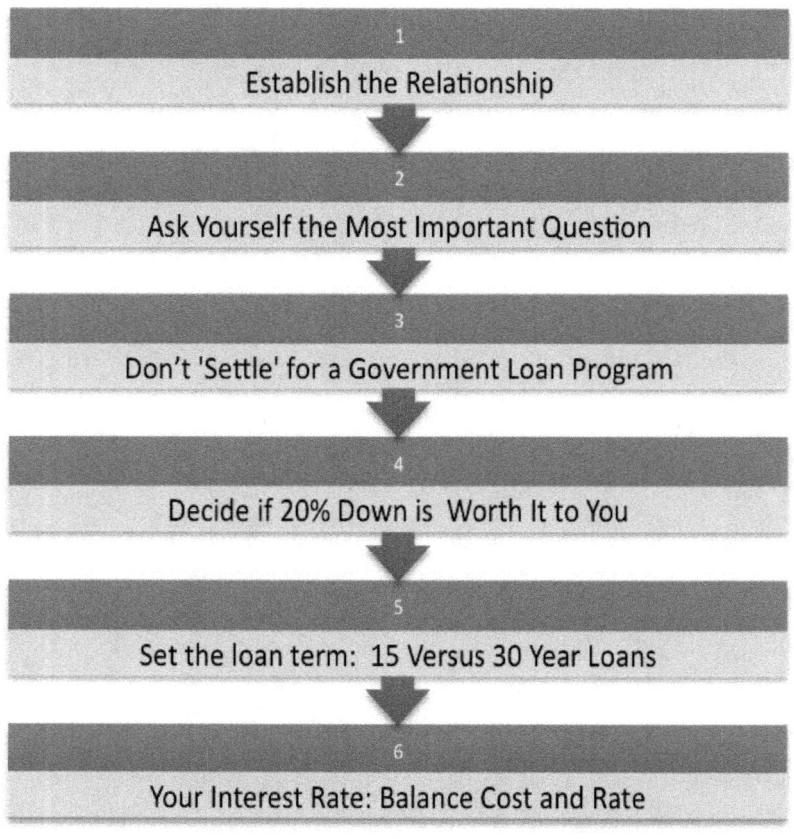

6-Step Mortgage Planning Process

The mortgage planning process is different from the typical "shopping around for a mortgage" experience. This defined system exists to ensure homebuyers integrate their mortgage into their overall short- and long-term financial goals.

Unfortunately, the vast majority of homebuyers only focus on one aspect of the mortgage planning process, the interest rate. While interest rates are certainly an important element of any mortgage plan, *they should always be the last item addressed.* You should never select an interest rate option before reviewing all the other facets of the mortgage plan.

It is absolutely critical to take the time to address every aspect of the mortgage planning process—because a "low" interest rate on the wrong mortgage loan can literally cost you thousands of dollars over the life of the loan.

When you follow the 6-Step Mortgage Planning Process, you will know for certain that you are making the absolute best decision for your financial future.

1. Establish the Relationship

When obtaining a mortgage loan, you must remember that this is a relationship, not just a transaction. As such, it requires a defined system of accountability to work effectively.

As a homebuyer, you're not interested in being "sold" a mortgage product. You're interested in receiving valuable financial advice and guidance. This comes from partnering with a mortgage lender who is committed, qualified and equipped to meet your needs. Establishing this relationship with your mortgage lender is the first step in the mortgage planning process.

Before proceeding with any mortgage plan, a mortgage lender needs to understand your personal financial goals. The mortgage lender should:

- Determine your financial situation and your timeframe for results and success.
- Gather all necessary documents before giving you any specific advice.
- Clearly explain the services they will provide to you.
- Explain how they are compensated for these services.

You, as a homebuyer, need to clearly explain how financial decisions are made in your household and include all the key decision makers in consultations with your mortgage lender. Also, be prepared to share personal and financial information with your mortgage lender to enable them to advise you on the best way to achieve your goals.

Only by analyzing your information and your current situation can a mortgage lender determine the best plan to meet your goals. Without this analysis, you and the mortgage lender cannot structure your mortgage correctly except by chance...

2. Ask Yourself the Most Important Question

When obtaining a mortgage, the most important question you need to ask yourself is:

How long will I carry this mortgage?

The answer to this question will guide you down the path to a successful mortgage plan.

When answering this question, consider things like starting a new family, changing jobs, continuing your education or having children move in or out of the home. *How long you will carry this mortgage will determine:*

- Whether you should pay points
- The best loan program for *you*
- The amount of your down payment, *and*
- The term of the loan

Any time you take out a new mortgage loan, remember to examine multiple interest rate options. These options should clearly illustrate the short- and long-term benefits coinciding with the available rates. Make sure you look at the following factors associated with each interest rate:

- Cash out-of-pocket
- Monthly payment
- The tax-deductible amount of the monthly payment

Then consider those items in conjunction with how long you are planning to carry this mortgage.

When I work with a client, I like to run a comparison over the length of time that they plan on carrying the mortgage that includes:

- The total amount they will pay on the mortgage with the different interest rate options
- Mortgage balance at specified time frames (5, 10, 20 years)
- Equity position at each of these points in time, and
- Tax savings over the duration of the loan

Lastly, I factor in upfront costs associated with the different interest rate options so you can make the best financial decision possible.

Remember, the option that makes the most financial sense always changes *based on the amount of time you plan to carry your mortgage.*

Discussed below are some of the factors affected by the most important question *how long will I likely carry this mortgage?*

Points

Rarely should you pay points upfront if you're not planning to carry the mortgage for more than 5 years. In many situations, paying points is counterproductive, and I encourage you to avoid paying any points by selecting an interest rate option where the lender pays points for you. (I'll explain how to accomplish this later, in "Closing Costs: Get the Bank to Pay Them.") **This way, you keep your money working for *you*.**

Fixed / ARM

There are a variety of loan programs, some very conservative and others more high-risk. A 30-year fixed mortgage with a consistent payment is a conservative approach, and, consequently, it bears a slightly higher interest rate. ARM (Adjustable Rate Mortgage) loans are going to represent a riskier option, due to the fact the interest rate is only fixed for a specified period. Obviously, the interest rates available through these riskier products are going to be lower than the more conservative options. In determining the best option for *you*, we revert to the primary question of how long you plan to carry this mortgage.

Plans to start a family within the next few years might mean you'll outgrow the house you are purchasing now; therefore, you might not have this loan for a long time. If you'll need to sell or refinance within 5 to 7 years, for any reason, (growing/shrinking family, expected job change, desired home improvements, or lower interest rates) you should choose a loan type that doesn't require you to pay points. In addition to avoiding points, spend time comparing the fixed rate options with ARM options. You might be pleasantly surprised at the choice that makes the most sense financially.

When interest rates are at historic lows, I advise my clients to lock in a 30-year mortgage, and even possibly pay points. When rates are higher, I play it more aggressively, advising my eligible clients to take out a 5, 7 or maybe even a 10-year adjustable rate mortgage, opting for no points. This is the opposite of what non-professionals tend to think, because most people believe they should take a conservative approach when rates are moving up (selecting a 30-year fixed mortgage). They don't understand that you should be aggressive when rates are *higher*, because of the greater possibility rates will improve in the future, allowing you to refinance out of this loan into a more conservative one.

Professionals know that interest rates are cyclical by nature, and historic lows dictate the more conservative approach. So, once again, understanding the all-prevailing question of how long you plan on carrying this mortgage can have a drastic impact on your overall financial situation, including paying points, choosing loan programs and saving or making the most money.

3. Don't 'Settle' for a Government Loan Program

One of the most important facets of the mortgage planning process is selecting the correct loan program. In most instances, this choice has more impact on your overall financial state than any other aspect of the loan. Each loan program has separate guidelines and requirements for down payment, upfront mortgage insurance, funding fees and monthly payments.

In today's mortgage environment, there are four standard loan programs available to homebuyers: Conventional, VA, Rural Development and FHA. The last three are all administered by the federal government in some way. These government programs can be intriguing to a homebuyer because they all permit low or zero down payments. However, each government loan has a specific set of requirements and fees applicable to the individual program. I'll discuss these programs first and then review Conventional loans.

VA Loans

These loans are administered through the Department of Veterans Administration. This program is available for military veterans and most active-duty military personnel. The greatest benefit of a VA loan is that no down payment is required. A homebuyer can purchase a home without spending a dollar out-of-pocket. Given this, almost all eligible homebuyers understandably assume this is obviously the right loan program for them.

Although I firmly believe in minimizing down payments to stay as liquid as possible, there is one major drawback to VA loans. They have an extremely expensive upfront "funding fee". This fee is charged to the homebuyer by the Veteran's Administration to guarantee the loan. (Essentially, this is a form of mortgage insurance.) The amount varies by the size of the loan and the number of times the homebuyer has utilized their VA loan eligibility. Disabled veterans are exempt from this funding fee. Normally, the funding fee is added to the loan amount. This means that most homebuyers taking out a VA loan actually owe more on their mortgage than their home is worth for the first few years.

VA FUNDING FEE

(FIRST-TIME USE)

HOME PURCHASE PRICE	$100,000
VA FUNDING FEE	$2,150
TOTAL LOAN AMOUNT	$102,150

VA FUNDING FEE

(ALL SUBSEQUENT USES)

HOME PURCHASE PRICE	$100,000
VA FUNDING FEE	$3,300
TOTAL LOAN AMOUNT	$103,300

Rural Development Loans

These loans are administered through the United States Department of Agriculture (USDA). In short, this loan program is designed to promote urban sprawl. Only homes located in a "rural development eligible area" can qualify for this loan program. This area is typically outside the city limits of most metropolitan areas. Like VA loans, Rural Development loans don't require a down payment.

Also, like the VA loan, Rural Development loans have an upfront funding fee (referred to as a Guarantee Fee). This fee varies based on the size of the loan and is normally factored back into the loan amount. Again, this typically puts most homebuyers into a negative equity position for the first couple of years. In addition to the upfront funding fee, Rural Development loans also require a monthly mortgage insurance payment. This payment directly increases the monthly payment of all Rural Development loans.

The Mortgage Book

RURAL DEVELOPMENT GUARANTEE FEE

Home Purchase Price	$100,000
Rural Development Guarantee Fee	$2,040
Total Loan Amount	$102,040

RURAL DEVELOPMENT MONTHLY MORTGAGE INSURANCE

(LOAN AMOUNT $102,040)

PAYMENT BREAKDOWN

(ASSUMING AN INTEREST RATE OF 5%)

Principal and Interest	$547.77
Taxes (Estimated)	$75.00
Insurance (Estimated)	$75.00
Mortgage Insurance	$38.82
Total Monthly payment	$736.59

FHA (Federal Housing Administration) Loans

FHA loans are administered through the Department of Federal Housing Administration. This loan program requires a minimum down payment of only 3.5 percent, all of which can be a gift to the homebuyer (many times coming from parents). There are limits to the amount you can borrow through an FHA loan, which vary from county to county. Almost all homes are eligible for an FHA mortgage. Similar to Rural Development loans, FHA loans require a combination of upfront mortgage insurance as well as a monthly mortgage insurance payment. Due to a recent insolvency facing the FHA, the cost for this monthly mortgage insurance has risen drastically.

FHA UPFRONT MORTGAGE INSURANCE

HOME PURCHASE PRICE	$100,000
DOWN PAYMENT	$3,500
LOAN AMOUNT	$96,500
UPFRONT MORTGAGE INSURANCE	$1,689
TOTAL LOAN AMOUNT	$98,188

The Mortgage Book

FHA MONTHLY MORTGAGE INSURANCE

(LOAN AMOUNT $98,188)

PAYMENT BREAKDOWN

(ASSUMING AN INTERST RATE OF 5%)

PRINCIPAL AND INTEREST	$527.09
TAXES (ESTIMATED)	$75.00
INSURANCE (ESTIMATED)	$75.00
MORTGAGE INSURANCE	$107.67
TOTAL MONTHLY PAYMENT	$784.76

Unfortunately, the FHA loan program has been branded the "first-time homebuyer" loan. True, in recent years more than 75% of FHA loans have gone to first-time homebuyers. However, it is not necessarily the best option for first-time buyers.

If you haven't been in the military, don't want to buy a home outside the city limits and do want to minimize your down payment, you may assume that an FHA loan is your only choice. This thought process is highly misguided, because you must consider the long-term costs associated with an FHA loan when choosing your mortgage plan. Simply put, the FHA loan option makes sense only when there is no alternative. Unfortunately, inexperienced lenders, by default, consistently recommend FHA loans.

Conventional Loans

Conventional loans are eventually purchased by Fannie Mae or Freddie Mac. For this reason, conventional loan products must meet the underlying terms and conditions they set forth. Conventional loans permit more flexibility, when structuring your mortgage, than any other program. They have no upfront funding fee or mortgage insurance premium and they do not require a monthly mortgage insurance premium.

Many people don't consider Conventional loan programs because they are under the misconception that a Conventional loan requires a down payment of 20 percent. **This is not true.**

If you don't make a 20 percent down payment, you will have to contend with mortgage insurance in some form or fashion. However, the mortgage insurance options available with a Conventional loan are financially more beneficial.

Many people also assume conventional loans require perfect credit. Again, this is false. Yes, there are some penalties for having less than perfect credit in the form of adjustments to your rate and fees. But these small adjustments pale in comparison to the mandated costs associated with other loan products.

The charts on the following pages more fully explain these concepts.

TRANSACTION COSTS
Closing Cost Impact

$250,000 Purchase Price 30 Year Fixed Mortgage	FHA 4.500%	VA 4.500%	Conv. 5.000%
Down Payment	$8,750	$0	$12,500
+ Closing Costs	$5,000	$5,000	$5,000
+ FHA / VA / USDA Fee	$3,500	$8,250	$0
− Financed Closing Fees	$3,500	$8,250	$0
− Seller Credit	$5,000	$5,000	$5,000
= Cash Needed to Close	$8,750	$0	$12,500
Cash Available	$50,000	$50,000	$50,000
Net Cash At Closing	$41,250	$50,000	$37,500

MONTHLY CASH FLOW
Payment Impact

$250,000 Purchase Price 30 Year Fixed Mortgage	FHA 4.500%	VA 4.500%	Conv. 5.000%
Total Borrowing	$244,750	$258,250	$237,500
Payment Comparison			
Interest Payment	$918	$968	$990
+ Principal Payment	$322	$341	$285
+ Taxes	$200	$200	$200
+ Insurance	$100	$100	$100
+ Mortgage Insurance	$275	$0	$0
= Pre-Tax Net Payment	$1,815	$1,609	$1,575
− Tax Savings	$279	$292	$297
= After-Tax Net Payment	$1,536	$1,317	$1,278
Payment Savings	$0	$219	$258

5 YEAR WEALTH IMPACT

$250,000 Purchase Price 30 Year Fixed Mortgage 7% Rate of Return	FHA 4.500%	VA 4.500%	Conv. 5.000%
Payments			
Monthly Mortgage	$1,815	$1,609	$1,575
Monthly Investment	$0	$219	$258
Initial Investment	$41,250	$50,000	$37,500
Annual Comparison			
House Value	$250,000	$250,000	$250,000
− Mortgage Liabilities	$223,109	$235,415	$218,093
= Equity	$26,891	$14,585	$31,907
− Payments	$150,157	$159,651	$147,477
− Cash Needed To Close	$8,750	$0	$12,500
+ Tax Savings	$16,191	$16,919	$17,273
+ Investment Balance	$58,477	$86,560	$71,632
= Cost	($57,348)	($41,587)	($39,165)
Savings Impact	$0	$15,760	$18,181

4. Decide if 20% Down is Worth It to You

The Down Payment

Many people ask whether 5%, 10%, 20% or even 30% is an appropriate down payment. They are seeking advice about whether less or more is better. There is no way to answer this question without taking a prudent look at your overall financial picture. To answer the question regarding how much you should put down, you need to ask yourself two questions:

1. *What do you actually have available for a down payment?*
2. *What would you do with this money if you didn't use it as a down payment?*

The easiest way to explain the impact of different down payments is through an example, so let's return to Sue and Dave. For this illustration, let's pretend Dave ended up taking out a 30-year mortgage at 4.75%.

Both Dave and Sue paid $250,000 to purchase their respective homes, but Dave put 20% down and Sue only put 5% down. Sue's interest rate is a quarter percent higher because she put less than 20% down. The after-tax monthly payment difference between the two options is $183.

Now let's assume that the day after closing, they both immediately start making investments that yield an annual 7% rate of return. Sue only put 5% down on her home, so she invests the $37,500 she didn't use as a down payment. Dave invests $183 a month, or the savings he received from putting more money down on his home.

After 15 years, the $37,500 Sue didn't use as a down payment has grown to $106,836. The $183 a month Dave invested has grown to $58,525. Assuming neither has paid any additional money towards the principal balance of their loan, Sue owes $161,224 on her mortgage, whereas Dave owes $134,129 on his mortgage. Now to compare these two options, subtract the balance of the investments from the mortgage owed. The 5% down payment option actually saved Sue more than $20,000, compared to Dave, and she now has $106,836 of liquid investments, compared to only $58,525 of liquid investments for Dave. Obviously, Sue owes more on her home; but is that really worth worrying about? Or is it true that she's put herself in a better financial position? Was 20% down really worth it in this scenario?

DOWN PAYMENT
Wealth Impact After 15 Years

$250,000 Purchase Price	20% Down	5% Down
House Value	$250,000	$250,000
− Mortgage Liability	$134,129	$161,224
= Equity	$115,871	$88,776
− Down Payment	$50,000	$12,500
− Payments	$220,916	$266,991
+ Tax Savings From Payments	$30,480	$38,304
+ Investment Balance After 7% Rate of Return	$58,525	$106,836
= Cost	($66,039)	($45,576)
Overall Savings	$0	$20,463

Mortgage Insurance

When you take out a conventional mortgage without putting at least 20% down, you must deal with mortgage insurance in some way. Most people don't realize they have options with mortgage insurance. How a loan originator handles mortgage insurance on a loan can have a drastic impact on the savings and financial state of customers over time. There are three standard ways to deal with mortgage insurance:

1. *Monthly Mortgage Insurance, the typical solution, offered to the borrower.* Your monthly mortgage payment includes principal, interest, taxes and insurance with mortgage insurance added on top. Facilitating mortgage insurance this way is usually *the least financially effective way* to deal with it. Ironically, this is the default many lenders advise. Normally, the only time this option makes sense is when you plan to carry the mortgage for a very short time.
2. *Upfront Mortgage Insurance.* With this option, the premium is paid upfront and not required again for the life of the loan. The premium is paid at closing and is included with the closing costs.
3. *Lender Pay Mortgage Insurance.* Here, the lender actually pays the mortgage insurance for the client and redeems the cost for it from the client in the form of either raising your interest rate slightly or by requiring you to pay points. (Remember Sue's

The Mortgage Book

interest rate was slightly higher because she didn't put 20% down).

MORTGAGE INSURANCE
Upfront Cost Breakdown

$250,000 Purchase Price 30 Year Fixed Mortgage	Monthly 4.000%	Upfront 4.000%	Lender Paid 4.250%
5% Down Payment	$12,500	$12,500	$12,500
+ Mortgage Insurance	$0	$3,800	$0
+ Closing Costs	$4,000	$4,000	$4,000
+ Prepaids	$3,000	$3,000	$3,000
− Seller Credit	$7,000	$7,000	$7,000
= Cash to Close	$12,500	$16,300	$12,500

MORTGAGE INSURANCE
Monthly Payment Breakdown

$250,000 Purchase Price 30 Year Fixed Mortgage	Monthly 4.000%	Upfront 4.000%	Lender Paid 4.250%
Interest Payment	$792	$792	$841
+ Principal Payment	$342	$342	$327
+ Estimated Taxes	$200	$200	$200
+ Estimated Insurance	$100	$100	$100
+ Mortgage Insurance	$158	$0	$0
= Pre-Tax Net Payment	$1,592	$1,434	$1,468
− Tax Savings	$248	$248	$260
= After-Tax Net Payment	$1,344	$1,186	$1,208

MORTGAGE INSURANCE
Overall Cost Over 10 Years

$250,000 Purchase Price 30 Year Fixed Mortgage	Monthly 4.000%	Upfront 4.000%	Lender Paid 4.250%
House Value	$250,000	$250,000	$250,000
− Mortgage Liabilities	$187,112	$187,112	$188,678
= Equity	$62,888	$62,888	$61,322
− Payments	$188,653	$172,063	$176,203
− Cash Needed To Close	$12,500	$16,300	$12,500
+ Tax Savings	$27,419	$27,419	$28,845
= Cost	($110,846)	($98,056)	($98,536)
Overall Savings	$0	$12,790	$12,311

As you can see, the way mortgage insurance is handled has significant effects on your future financial state. In most situations, paying mortgage insurance on a monthly basis does not make sense. If you plan to carry the mortgage for an extended time, I recommend either the upfront mortgage insurance or lender paid mortgage insurance. Since both of these have inherent upfront costs, they can be included with the closing costs, and therefore you might even be able to negotiate for the seller to pay these costs for you. Imagine that! Get a conventional mortgage, without putting 20% down, and not having to pay for any of your mortgage insurance costs. That's what a properly structured mortgage can do for you!

5. Set the Loan Term: 15 versus 30 Year Loans

For some clients, a 15-year payment plan does work best, particularly if they are less than 30 years away from retirement. I rarely advise a client to take out a 15-year loan, but sometimes it does make sense. Make sure you're working with someone who understands your needs and your goals, and can provide intelligent options for you to review. It's important to remember:

You can turn a 30-year loan into a 15,
but you can't turn a 15-year loan into a 30.

A 15-year mortgage carries a lower interest rate than a 30-year mortgage, and therefore reduces the overall cost of the money that you're borrowing over that period. However, understand that:

A 15-year mortgage amortizes over half the time,
resulting in a significantly higher monthly payment.

It's important to assess whether that payment will ever be a problem, so you need to consider potential issues involving your income in the future. Be sure you want to obligate yourself to that elevated payment, because that's exactly what the 15-year mortgage loan represents -- an *obligation* to a higher monthly payment.

You should also remember that you can always convert a 30-year loan into a 15-year loan by prepaying the principal correctly. But you cannot convert a 15-year loan into a 30-year loan. That's why it is so important to ensure you'll be comfortable with the higher payment in the future.

I like to recommend 15-year loans in some very specific cases where they can help you meet your short- and long-term financial goals better than a 30-year loan. Again, this is another example of why you need to work with a mortgage lender who reviews your overall financial picture when structuring your mortgage. For example, if someone is within 15 years of retirement, I might recommend a 15-year loan, because they're going to be switching to a fixed income. Putting someone in a 30-year loan when they can obviously afford a 15-year payment and are approaching retirement might be counterproductive to meeting their specific goals. A 50-year-old entering a 30-year loan won't be debt-free by the age of retirement at

The Mortgage Book

65. If that's their objective, then a 30-year loan isn't the right choice for them.

Make sure your lender puts together a comprehensive spreadsheet for you to review, showing you the difference in payments between a 30-year and 15-year mortgage. They should also review where you'd be in the future as far as your equity position, debt-free status and out-of-pocket expenses over those time periods. By taking these steps, you can be sure you're making the best decision as you consider financing your future.

Many people contemplate a 15-year loan when they should not. For example, I recently completed a refinance transaction with a client. Six months before we closed on this transaction, he had actually refinanced from a 30-year mortgage down to a 15-year mortgage with a nearby lending institution. However, when that lender did his refinance, *they didn't consider his <u>overall financial state.</u>*

When he refinanced with them, my client went from a 30-year loan to a 15-year loan, seeking to pay his house off early. Unfortunately, the other lender did not discuss my client's $35,000 in credit card debt! He was paying 17.5% interest on this money every month. Without professional advice, he chose a 15-year loan to pay his home off quicker when he was making the minimum monthly payment on those credit cards.

When you take a holistic financial approach to this specific client's situation, you see he obviously needed to attack his credit card debt first, eliminating that high, non-deductible interest, *before* restructuring his home loan. Six months after he refinanced with the other bank, I refinanced him back into a 30-year loan, took cash out of the equity of his house, paid off the credit card debt in full, and got him back on track to pay the house off in 15 to 20 years. At the same time, we structured his loan so that he now has a smaller minimum monthly mortgage payment to ensure he never has to drop back into credit card debt.

Unlike the other bank, I took the holistic financial approach and substantially improved my client's financial position moving forward. This is what can happen when you work with a mortgage professional who understands how a mortgage can benefit your overall financial life.

6. Your Interest Rate - Balance Cost and Rate

Any time you consider taking out a new mortgage, it is important to look at three fundamental areas. These three areas should always be addressed during the last step of mortgage planning process.

1. *Does this make sense for me today?* When comparing different mortgage loan options, what will it cost you *today* to achieve a specific interest rate option? Please remember, it's always a balance between cost and rate. You can get a loan where you pay nothing to the bank, or you can even get a loan where the bank is paying you. Paying something isn't necessarily bad, as long as you can clearly see a benefit over time; the lowest interest rate isn't always the best option. This is, once again, why we need to ask how long you're going to carry the mortgage. For a loan you plan to carry for a short period, it typically makes more sense to avoid upfront costs. Don't just look at the rate; consider the costs as well.

2. *Does this make sense from a monthly perspective?* With each interest rate option, consider how much

your monthly payments will be in the context of your financial future. This is an important factor, since you will be living with this payment for many years. Be certain to consider your entire financial picture before making a decision in this area.

3. *Does this make sense for me over time?* This is what most people miss, and it is BIG. This will show you, based on the mortgage plan and the in-depth structures and interest rates available, which mortgage scenario best meets your specific needs.

By minimizing the down payment and structuring the mortgage properly, I've seen the mortgage planning process save clients thousands of dollars and position themselves in a much better overall financial situation.

This is the 6-Step Mortgage Planning Process you should follow to obtain the best mortgage for your unique situation. Can you now see why answering that one simple question (Step 2 in the process—"How long will I carry this loan?") is really the starting place when you are considering buying a home? Don't be lured into a mortgage simply because of a low interest rate. Walk through the mortgage planning process and maintain control of your money!

Lee's Mortgage Formula

The formula I typically use when comparing different mortgage options is this: over the amount of time you plan to carry the mortgage, take the value of the home and subtract the projected mortgage balance (at the specified future date) to determine your equity position. Now, to compare different loan options, subtract the amount you brought to closing (your upfront, out-of-pocket expense). Then subtract the amount you paid on the mortgage over the specified period. Finally, add in the tax savings over this period.

The Mortgage Book

With interested clients, I explain even more thoroughly and illustrate what happens when they put those dollars that they *didn't* put down on the home, as well as the monthly payment difference, into an investment with a conservative rate of return. This allows them to see just how much the right mortgage strategy can influence every area of their financial life. By following the mortgage planning process, you'll have the information you need to make the best decision for your future.

The Mortgage Book

By doing this math, we can strategically determine the right option for *you,* based on the amount of time that you plan on carrying the mortgage. Make sure that you're working with someone who takes the time to discuss all these options, to ensure you choose the right scenario for your specific circumstance. Shortcutting this process could cost you thousands of dollars over the life of your mortgage.

OTHER FACTORS

THAT CAN AFFECT

THE MORTGAGE PLANNING PROCESS

In this section, I'll explain various factors that affect the mortgage planning process. It's important to know and understand these factors as you seek to structure your mortgage in the most beneficial way.

Emotional Factors: Is this a House or a Home?

Many decisions are based on emotion, but you really need to step back and remove emotion from the mortgage planning equation. Your property can be one of your best financial tools going forward, so you need to take the emotion *out* of buying or refinancing a property. It may be your *home*, but you are purchasing or refinancing a *house*.

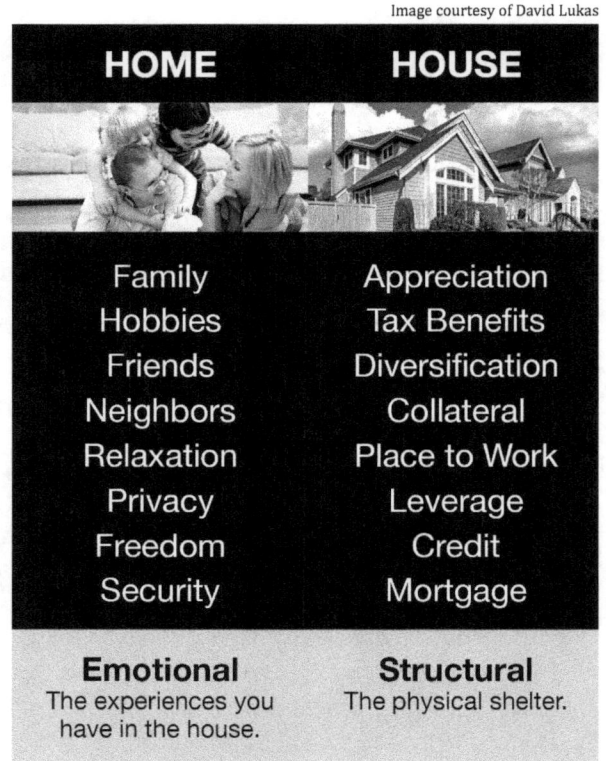

Image courtesy of David Lukas

The Mortgage Book

Your house is an investment that can help you build wealth and create financial security for your family. Your home is where you live and entertain. They are both part of the property that you are purchasing. By understanding this difference, you'll be able to separate the emotional aspects of owning a home from the financial aspects of buying a house.

Credit Score

Over the course of a mortgage loan, the amount of interest paid can add up to hundreds of thousands of dollars. The most significant determinant of your interest rate options is your credit score. The higher your credit score, the lower the interest rate options available to you. Now more than ever, a good credit score is vital to having access to the best interest rate options.

Your credit score is a number that expresses your credit worthiness. Your lender will use three different credit-reporting agencies: Experian, TransUnion and Equifax, to help determine your ability to repay your mortgage loan.

These credit-reporting agencies collect financial information about everyone with a Social Security number. They process that information with a system developed by the Fair Isaac Corporation (FICO) to calculate your credit score and determine your credit-worthiness. Although the tiers for credit scoring go up to 850 on the FICO scale, typically a score of 740 or more will qualify you for the best interest rate options available.

Your FICO score will range between 300 and 850. Since each of the three credit reporting agencies collect information independently of each other, you can have three different credit scores on your credit report. A FICO score considers five different factors. Below is a list of the factors, the percentage of your score based on that factor and a general synopsis of each one.

The 5 Components of Your Credit Score

1. Payment History (35%)

It is <u>essential</u> to pay your credit bills on time. Your score drops significantly with every instance of:
- a 30 days late payment
- collection activity
- financial judgment, or

- Bankruptcy

2. Amount You Owe Compared to Balances (30%)

Your available credit compared to the amount owed. It's a good rule-of-thumb to be at 30% or less of your available revolving credit lines.

3. Length of Credit History (15%)

Easy rule-of-thumb: the longer your accounts are open, the more positive impact it has on your overall credit score. In fact, if you have a card that is over 10 years old with even a little activity, it's best to keep that account open.

4. Mix of Credit (10%)

There is no specific rule-of-thumb in this category, but having different types of credit demonstrate credit-worthiness. If you have loans, such as a car loan, and open credit cards, the mix helps prove your experience borrowing and repaying money (versus a concentration of credit cards only).

5. New Credit Applications (10%)

It can hurt your credit score to have multiple reports pulled by potential creditors in a short amount of time. (However, there is a model that compensates for people shopping rates on home and car loans.)

Your credit score is a major influence in the mortgage planning process. You should work diligently to keep your score as high as possible so you can gain maximum benefit for your financial future.

I suggest sitting down with a qualified lender, to analyze your credit, well before making a strategic decision to move forward with purchasing or refinancing a property.

The Best Interest Rate

Many consumers, understandably, think the most important part of finding the right mortgage is finding the *lowest interest rate* available. The interest rate is certainly an important component of the mortgage and, obviously, achieving a great rate should be one of your goals. However, how do you accomplish this? Before purchasing a home, you should understand a few things about rates.

Low, fixed mortgage rates are determined by mortgage-backed securities, which trade daily on the Chicago Board of Trade. This is very similar to the way stocks trade on the NASDAQ and the Dow. Just like stock prices, mortgage rates change weekly, daily and even hourly. That's why obtaining the lowest rate can be somewhat elusive, just as Dave discovered in our opening story. Instead of searching for the mortgage professional who could properly advise him about the correct time to lock in his interest rate, Dave did what most homebuyers do - he just went blindly with the lowest rate he could find.

Suppose you choose to lock in your rate. One day before your loan closes, the bond market rallies, and mortgage rates drop a quarter of a percent. Have you really obtained the lowest interest rate? *Does it matter?* What would you do differently? Are you going to stop the entire process, delay your closing, and switch lenders to get this new lower interest rate, with the possibility this same scenario will reoccur?

Then, two days after your loan closes, interest rates drop even further; have you achieved the lowest interest rate available now? The answer, of course, is "No." In reality, mortgage rates are affected by many factors within the economy. If I, or anyone else, knew the exact hour and day rates would be at their very lowest, we would be very rich. We probably wouldn't be in the mortgage business anymore, and I, personally, would be on a beach in Florida.

As you can see, achieving the lowest rate can be challenging. Therefore, your best move is to ask around and find someone who understands the dynamics of the mortgage market, and can help you decide when to strategically lock-in your interest rate. In financing your largest asset, you should always work with a trusted mortgage professional. Make sure your lender can:

- access live, real-time mortgage bond quotes
- explain the intricacies of mortgage bond and interest rate real-time movements
- warn you of costly intraday pricing movements

Working with a mortgage lender who cannot explain the particulars of interest rate movement is equivalent to working with a financial advisor who can't explain why stock prices go up or down.

If Dave had stopped and listened to Sue's lender, he still might have taken on a 15-year loan, but at a minimum he would have locked in his interest rate that Thursday afternoon, knowing the Jobs Report was coming out the following morning.

The Mortgage Book

I have seen people obsess over getting the lowest rate only to miss the boat; and even if you obtain the lowest rate, this is only one piece of the puzzle. There are many factors to consider in addition to the interest rate. Always remember:

A great rate on the wrong mortgage strategy can <u>literally</u> cost you tens of thousands of dollars over the life of the loan.

When making the decision to lock in your interest rate, you must understand that there's always a balance between cost and rate. How long you plan to carry your mortgage will determine what interest rate is best for you; therefore, <u>the lowest interest rate is not always the best option</u>.

Several times a week, my phone rings with an interest rate shopper, like Dave, at the end of the line.

"What's your rate today on a 30-year fixed mortgage?" is the most frequent question.

"What would you like it to be?" is the response I use most of time.

Obviously, this typically throws people for a loop. After a few seconds of silence, my latest "Dave" comes back with,

"Well, what do you mean exactly? Do I get to pick whatever interest rate I want with you?"

This is when I take the opportunity to educate "Dave" on how interest rates work.

Getting the lowest interest rate is not always the best decision.

When you're shopping around and ultimately looking at locking in your interest rate, it's important to factor in all of the variables, including what it will cost you today to achieve that specific interest rate. Please remember; **it's always a balance between cost and rate.**

You can get a loan where you pay nothing to the bank. You can even take out a loan where you not only pay nothing to the bank, but the bank actually gives *you* a lender credit to pay for all of your other third-party costs, such as title, appraisal, taxes, etc. In other words, we (the bank) are paying you to take out a loan with us – it sounds crazy, but it's true! If you can clearly benefit from this type of arrangement *over time*, it might be the best option for you.

The lowest interest rate isn't always the best option, because it is extremely important to factor in how long you plan to carry this mortgage. Typically speaking, the less time you will be in this house, the less sense it makes to pay upfront fees in exchange for a lower rate. However, if you're planning to pay on your mortgage for an extended period of time, then it may make sense to pay upfront costs to secure that lower interest rate. The most important thing is to ensure you evaluate multiple interest rate options and lock in the option that makes the most financial sense *over the length of time you actually plan to carry the mortgage.*

Many people unknowingly make an unwise decision to pay upfront costs to get a lower rate. Since your mortgage is such a large component of your financial life, it is crucial that you ask around and find a loan professional who considers your overall long- and short-term financial goals.

A professional mortgage planner would love to sit down and talk with you about the many factors that go into these decisions. It shouldn't cost you a penny to assess your options. When I go through a comprehensive mortgage planning consultation with a prospective borrower, I certainly don't charge anything. A true professional should be willing to do this for you. It's my firm conviction that once you have met with a lender that educates you on the critical topics discussed thus far, you will know you've made the right decision to entrust them with your mortgage.

Why Do Rates Change?

Interest rates move on a daily basis due to the ebb and flow of mortgage-backed security bonds. As mortgage-backed securities trade, they fluctuate based on economic developments, including the stock market and a variety of economic factors. This is why it's difficult to get the "lowest interest rate"; there is enormous volatility tied to mortgage rates.

The Stock Market

First, the stock market has a dynamic relationship with the trading of mortgage-backed securities. Typically, when stocks are selling off (prices falling), mortgage-backed securities are rallying, and vice versa. How does this affect rates? *When mortgage-backed security prices rise, home loan rates move lower; when they fall, home loan rates rise.*

Economic Factors and Reports

Other factors affecting each trading session include economic data that affects all capital markets, including mortgage-backed securities. Some important economic reports that come out on a monthly basis and affect mortgage rates are:

- Unemployment claims
- Government employment reports for non-farm payrolls
- Inflation ratings
- Reports on the nation's manufacturing
- Gross Domestic Product (GDP) report
- Retail sales, and

- Consumer sentiment

As a rule-of-thumb, positive economic reports tend to push the price of bonds lower and favor the stock market, therefore mortgage interest rates rise.

The Federal Reserve versus the Stock Market

The media does a disgraceful job of educating consumers on the Federal Reserve. When you hear "The Fed lowered interest rates," you can be sure the phones in my office will begin ringing, because everybody thinks that means mortgage rates have fallen. More often than not, the *opposite* has actually occurred.

First, NORMALLY, **the Federal Reserve has absolutely no direct impact on mortgage interest rates**. The Federal Reserve (The Fed) controls:

- the short term overnight lending rate,
- the Fed funds rate, and
- the discount rate.

Each of these has a very close relationship to the Prime Rate. *In normal economic times, when The Fed lowers their benchmark interest rates, mortgage rates tend to*

The Mortgage Book

move higher, and vice versa. Why is this? It's simply a matter of investor cash movement from lower return financial instruments to higher return investments.

This means the stock market has an equal or greater impact on mortgage interest rates than the Federal Reserve. Mortgage interest rates fluctuate based on the trading of mortgage-backed securities. Typically, the money going into stocks is coming out of bonds and mortgage-backed securities to fund the purchase of stocks. When the stock market is selling off, money is coming out of stocks, and needs somewhere to go. Often, since they can generate a guaranteed yield, the money is put into mortgage-backed securities. *When money goes into bonds or mortgage-backed securities, mortgage rates come down; when mortgage-backed securities are sold to generate cash flow for investments in stock, rates go up.* This means the more accurate, dynamic relationship is between mortgage-backed securities and stocks, *not* the Federal Reserve.

In summary, when The Federal Reserve lowers rates, stocks rally (rise), causing mortgage-backed securities to sell off, resulting in *rising mortgage rates.*

This is the dynamic you need to understand and watch carefully.

However, it's not always a clear-cut formula. That's why it's important for you to work with a mortgage professional who not only understands these different aspects, but also what causes rates to go up and down. It could save you thousands of dollars and many headaches.

The Lender's Compensation

Lenders make money on a mortgage transaction in the following ways:

First, they keep the fees collected upfront at the time of closing. These fees are sometimes referred to as points and/or bank fees, but they should be called "Origination Charges." This is what the lender is charging you to originate your mortgage.

Second, they receive a premium when they sell the right to service your loan. Most of the time, regardless of where you get your mortgage, that company will not "keep" your mortgage on their books. They will sell it to another company, who will then "service" your mortgage

The Mortgage Book

for a number of years. This is very common, and not something you need to be concerned about. It doesn't affect you in any way. This servicing company is simply a pass thru. The servicer will keep a small percentage of the interest from each month's payment in exchange for handling customer support. Ultimately, all loans end up with Fannie Mae, Freddie Mac or Ginnie Mae.

Those are the only 2 ways that lenders earn money when it comes to mortgage loans. You need to understand this to make the best decisions for your financial future. The bank's objective is to earn money from the money they lend. As a borrower, your objective is to keep your money working for *you*, not the bank. Having the proper mortgage strategy can help you maintain control of your money so you'll have greater liquidity and more security.

Planning to Prepay Your Mortgage

Prepaying your mortgage can be a bad idea. If you can earn more through investing than what you're paying on your mortgage after taxes, why would you take away that ability by prepaying on your mortgage loan?

MORTGAGE INTEREST RATE	5%	INVESTMENT RETURN	5%
LESS TAX SAVINGS (25% BRACKET)	1.25%	vs. CAPITAL GAINS TAX (15%)	.75%
AFTER-TAX MORTGAGE COST	3.75%	AFTER-TAX PROFIT	4.25%

If the interest rate on your house is 5% and you are in the 25% marginal tax bracket, then the after-tax interest rate on your home loan is actually 3.75%. That's because 25% of your mortgage interest is deductible (based on your tax bracket.) In this case, that's equal to 1.25% of your interest rate.

If you can take the money you would typically prepay on your home loan and, instead, put it to work earning more than 3.75%, why would you ever prepay on your home loan? This concept is something that Sue, from our story, understood completely. By putting her dollars to work <u>outside</u> of her mortgage, instead of dumping them into the equity of her home, she put herself in a significantly better overall financial position.

The Effect of Time

Mortgage payments get easier over time. Having a mortgage can actually get to be fun, yes, fun! My grandfather used to love talking about his mortgage payment -- all $96.00-a-month of it. You see, he and my grandma bought their first home in 1955 for a whopping price of $16,000. My granddad used to tell me how, at the time, he thought it was crazy.

"How in the world was I going to the handle such a huge mortgage payment?" He'd say.

After all, my granddad was earning less than $3,000 a year back then. Spending almost $1,200 a year on mortgage payments was nuts, he thought. Of course, by the seventies, granddad was laughing about it. Why? Because his payment was identical to what it was when he took out the loan, yet his income had steadily risen. Thus, his mortgage payment had become insignificant when compared to his income. Furthermore, the value of his home had increased substantially.

When you first purchase a home, you might struggle a bit to make your mortgage payment, but over time, that payment becomes easier, because it is relative to your income (especially if you have a fixed-rate loan). Those payments never go up, but, typically, your income does. That's why it can be fun to have a mortgage. Just ask my granddad!

The Effect of T-I-M-E

Undoubtedly, the primary motive for people seeking a shorter-term mortgage is to pay their house off earlier, to eliminate the monthly expense associated with their home. What they don't realize, though, is that <u>the payment on your home never completely goes away</u>. The reason is that time keeps on ticking. And when I say TIME, I mean—

> Taxes,
>
> Insurance,
>
> Maintenance, and
>
> Expenses.

You may pay off your home loan, but you have to continue paying real estate taxes. You don't want to own a property without insurance on it; and anyone who has owned a property in the past knows that the maintenance and expenses on a home never go away. Some people spend so much time and energy trying to get their house paid off early that they forget how time keeps on ticking. By remembering T-I-M-E, they'll realize they're always going to have monthly housing costs, whether they have a loan against the house or not.

The Equity Factor

It's imperative that homeowners remember this:

The size of your mortgage doesn't affect your home's value.

Over time, the amount of equity you have in your home is determined *less* by the size of your mortgage, and *more* by appreciation and depreciation. Furthermore, the equity you have in the property is not liquid; when you need it most, it is difficult to access.

Equity is the difference between what your home is currently worth, based on its appraised value, and the amount you still owe on it. What you owe on your home is completely irrelevant to your home's value. Equity may look good on paper, but it's not easily accessible in an emergency. This is why it's critical that you maintain control of your money and fully understand the ramifications of *building up equity* instead of *maintaining liquidity*.

To obtain a mortgage or home equity loan, you must prove your ability to repay the loan. If you're in a situation that has prompted a need to access the equity in your home, there is a high probability you're having income difficulties. This is going to make it difficult, and perhaps impossible, to access those dollars stored in the equity of your home. Don't use your home as a bank and store money in it. Against popular belief, it's not the safe financial thing to do. Just ask Dave, from our story earlier.

Six months before I wrote this book, a couple approached me. I had originated a mortgage for one of their friends two years ago, and their friend had given them my name. This couple had a dilemma. The wife was a stay-at-home mom, and the company the husband had worked for over the last 20 years had just shut down. Their daughter was getting married in a month, and this couple had been saving up for the wedding expenses by paying extra on their mortgage loan.

Over the past 15 years, they had paid an extra $30,000 on the principal of the home loan, which they had planned to use for the wedding. They had figured they'd just keep paying extra on the mortgage, and when the wedding day arrived, they'd pull the money back out. Disappointingly, I could do nothing for this couple. At this moment in time, they had no documentable income to prove their ability to repay a new mortgage loan. They eventually chose to spread the wedding expenses across four different credit cards, which cost them thousands of extra dollars in high and non-tax-deductible interest.

You're buying a home because you think it will rise in value. If you didn't think so, you would probably choose to rent. Your home's eventual rise or fall in value will occur whether you have a mortgage on it or not. So go ahead and get a mortgage; your home's value will not be affected. That's why owning your home outright is like having money buried under a mattress. Any equity you have in the house is earning no interest, and it is not easy to

The Mortgage Book

access. You wouldn't stuff $10,000 under your mattress, so why put $400,000 in the walls of your house? Having a long-term mortgage lets your equity grow while your home's value grows.

Everyone wants to build equity; it's a primary financial reason for owning a house. It can help pay for college, weddings, retirement, toys, etc. But even more important than building equity, is maintaining your ability to repay a mortgage or home equity loan.

Many people say that having a mortgage is a bad idea because the bigger the mortgage, the lower your equity. *They're <u>wrong</u>, and the following example explains why.*

Let's say you buy a house for $300,000 and you get a $250,000, 30-year mortgage. Your down payment in this situation is $50,000, thus you begin with $50,000 in equity.

Like most homeowners, you want that equity to grow, grow, grow. By making your payments every month, your loan balance in 20 years will be $126,000 ($250,000 loan less $126,000 remaining balance = $124,000 new equity); you've added $124,000 to your equity position. This supports the contention that equity grows as you pay off the mortgage, and that the faster you pay off the mortgage, the faster your equity will grow.

However, this thinking fails to acknowledge that this is not the only way to build equity in your house. Your house will almost certainly grow in value over the next 20 years. If it rises in value at a rate of 3% per year, it will be worth $542,000 in 20 years. You'll have nearly a quarter of a million dollars in new equity, even if your principal balance wasn't paid down another cent.

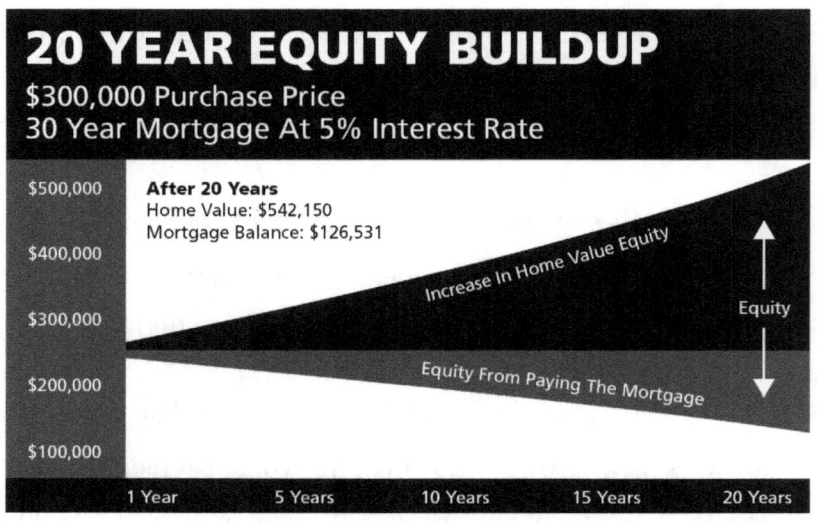

As you can see, it's essential to understand the difference between having a *mortgage* and having *equity*.

Real Estate Contract Negotiations

One of the most important facets of purchasing a home is talking to your mortgage professional *before* writing an offer on the property. The reason for this is:

The way you structure your real estate purchase contract is crucial to how you structure your loan.

The Realtors I work with routinely call me when submitting an offer, to ensure the purchase contract meets all my requirements related to structuring the loan for our mutual client.

There are many moving parts associated with a purchase loan. You want to ensure the purchase contract is structured in a way that allows you to stay within your comfort level with regard to out-of-pocket expenses at closing *and* monthly payment expenses. For these reasons, purchasing the home for the cheapest dollar amount is not always the goal when negotiating a purchase contract

If you're going to take out a home loan against the property you are purchasing, *the Realtor involved in a purchase transaction shouldn't be the only person structuring the offer on the house; your mortgage lender should be just as involved in the transaction.* This is because the way your mortgage is structured will have more far-reaching implications related to your overall financial health than the actual purchase price the Realtor has negotiated. You'll want to make sure you're working with someone who understands these concepts, so that any offer you make puts you in the best financial position for your specific situation.

Always consult an experienced mortgage professional before making an offer on a house.

Pay More for the House

Sometimes, it's better to pay *more* for a house. When purchasing a new home, most people fixate on the purchase price, when really they need to evaluate their overall financial picture and how long they're going to be in the property.

When should you pay more for a house? Let me show you an example of two people buying an identical house in the same neighborhood.

The Mortgage Book

Let's introduce Aggressive Abby, who is buying a house for $300,000 and gets the seller to pay $10,000 of her closing costs. Her friend, Bashful Bobby, buys an identical house for $290,000 but doesn't get the seller to pay any of his closing costs. They each elect to make a 20% down payment -- $60,000 for Abby and $68,000 for Bobby. (*Remember*: *the mortgage amount doesn't affect the value of the house.*)

Both Abby and Bobby had $100,000 available for their home purchases. But Abby only had to bring $60,000 to closing, leaving $40,000 liquid. Bobby had to bring $68,000 to closing because, although he bought his house for less, he did not require the seller to pay any of his closing costs. Consequently, he now has a lower liquid cash position (by $8,000). You would think their monthly payments would be considerably different, since Abby paid $10,000 more for her house than Bobby did. However, both Abby and Bobby are in the 25% marginal tax bracket, so after taking their tax implications into effect (how much interest will be tax-deductible based on their marginal tax rate); Abby's monthly payment is only $32.00 higher than Bobby's. And she bought the house for $10,000 *more*.

Over a 15-year period, Abby is actually going to save $11,863 compared to Bobby, despite the higher price she paid.

PURCHASE PRICE
Wealth Impact After 15 Years

30 Year Fixed Mortgage 7% Rate of Return	$300,000	$290,000
Payments		
Minimum Monthly Mortgage	$1,288	$1,245
One Time Investment	$40,000	$32,000
Comparison		
House Value	$300,000	$300,000
− Mortgage Liability	$162,921	$157,491
= Equity	$137,079	$142,509
− Payments	$271,907	$256,177
− Cash Needed To Close	$60,000	$68,000
+ Tax Savings	$51,093	$49,390
+ Investment Balance	$113,958	$90,638
= Cost	($29,777)	($41,640)
Overall Savings	$11,863	$0

Don't fixate on the purchase price; the house will be worth the same regardless of the mortgage. **Don't reduce your liquid assets by paying costs at closing when the seller (or the bank) can pay those costs for**

you. *The way your mortgage is structured is more important than the purchase price!*

Another subtle benefit of buying your home for a higher purchase price is that you are actually helping the neighborhood as far as housing values are concerned. Real estate values are determined by comparable homes currently on the market and those that have actually sold in recent months. When you pay more for a house, you are actually helping to increase the value of the homes in your neighborhood. If everyone in the neighborhood used this clever tactic, you would certainly build equity faster.

Tax Deductions for Mortgage Interest

Most likely, mortgages are the cheapest money you will ever borrow. Lenders *qualify* you for a mortgage loan when you demonstrate your ability to repay it. Then the question becomes, "How much interest will you have to pay to obtain that loan?"

The greater the lender's confidence in getting its money back, the less interest it will charge you. By offering your house as collateral, you agree to let the bank have your home if you don't repay the loan. This collateral drastically reduces the bank's risk, resulting in a very low interest rate compared to credit cards, car loans, and so forth. Since VISA® can't take (and doesn't want) the sweater you charged if you don't pay the bill, they charge a higher interest rate. Credit card companies know that a certain portion of their cardholders will not pay their bill, so they charge extremely high interest rates to most cardholders to make up for the risk and financial loss due to those who will default on their payments. That's not a bad business plan, but it doesn't benefit the cardholder. Furthermore, unlike mortgage interest, the interest on these other forms of credit is not tax-deductible.

Mortgage interest is tax-deductible, and tax favorable. These two points are related, and offer important benefits to carrying a mortgage. The interest you pay on loans acquired on your residence is tax-deductible. The deduction is taken at your top tax bracket; thus, if you're in the 35% tax bracket, every dollar you pay in mortgage interest saves you 35¢ in federal income taxes. You can also save on state income taxes as well.

When structuring your mortgage loan, you need to look beyond different interest rates, fees and terms; dig deeper and analyze the tax advantages/disadvantages of each structuring option. It's not as simple as "What's your rate?" This is especially true for people in a higher marginal tax bracket; they really need to look at the interest rate and how the mortgage interest tax-deductibility will affect their financial state. You should combine this tax thinking with all your other financial goals when planning the structure of your mortgage loan. And, always remember:

The value of your house is not determined by the size of your mortgage.

Closing Costs: Get the Bank to Pay Them

How do you get the bank to pay your closing costs? It's very simple: the lender gives you an interest rate that generates a rebate to them, no different from the one they receive when they execute a loan for you with no origination charges. You may be asking, "How does the lender make money if they're making a loan with no closing fees?" The answer is, when the lender originating your loan sells the servicing of the loan, the purchasing institution pays them a rebate that they allocate toward your closing costs, thereby paying all of your closing costs for you. Yes, you have to pay a slightly higher interest rate than if you had paid points and fees, but remember, the interest rate is **_not_** the most important factor—how long you'll carry this loan is. Your interest rate will be approximately a quarter of a percent above market rates, but it costs you nothing to get this loan and it will cost you nothing to take advantage of lower interest rate options in the future. This allows you to maximize your cash and minimize your interest expense simultaneously. If interest rates move lower in the future, it will be much easier to take advantage of refinancing if you don't have to recover any prior closing costs. Keeping that in mind, you always need to watch interest rates in the future. When you have an opportunity to refinance your loan for free, (with the lender paying all of your closing costs and fees) you can take advantage and be aggressive. It's all part of managing your overall financial health.

Please understand that these "no cost" loans benefit you greatly. In the future, when rates adjust downward, you can do this again and again and again, with absolutely no cost to you, while lowering your interest rate each time. With loans like these, each time you refinance your loan amount stays exactly the same, but your monthly payment goes down. This is just one more strategy good mortgage lenders use with their clients to help them maximize wealth through their mortgage. The best part is that it doesn't cost you a penny to implement it.

Debt Consolidation

Let's recall the client who had refinanced his mortgage from a 30-year to a 15-year note, with the desire to pay his house off early. The home was worth $350,000, he owed $190,000 on it, and he also owed $35,000 in high-interest credit card debt. The loan officer who did his first refinance hadn't even mentioned using the equity in his home to pay off those credit cards. Unfortunately, the focus was solely on reducing the interest rate and paying the house off early. The loan officer didn't take the holistic financial approach I believe is required when formulating a mortgage plan. I witness loan officers doing this all the time, and *it should be a crime*.

For this client, we completed a new refinance, dropped his total monthly outlay by over $900, and got him on track to pay his house off in less than 20 years. I did this with a higher interest rate option than his current mortgage. The client was rather hesitant at first, wondering why he should refinance into a *higher* interest rate. By showing him that his mortgage was a financial tool, at his disposal to help accomplish other things in life, he quickly realized that **he was under the typical misconception that refinancing is pointless if your interest rate is going to be higher.** However, I was able to show him that, even with the higher interest rate, we could save him over $900 a month.

Points

Points are not as confusing as many assume. They are nothing more than upfront fees that you pay to buy yourself a more attractive interest rate. By paying this additional money as a part of your closing costs, you will generate a lower interest rate, and subsequently a lower monthly payment. Contrary to popular opinion, points are not the only way a mortgage lender (or I, as a loan originator) gets paid. No-point loans are not unusual and originators/lenders would not facilitate them if points were the only way they were paid. If you're willing to pay points, you can benefit from a lower interest rate and a resulting lower payment. But before you can make that determination, you'll need to decide *how long you'll need to carry this mortgage*, to make sure that paying points is the best option for you.

During the last step of the mortgage planning process, an extensive evaluation needs to occur, regarding the topic of paying points. Along with your mortgage lender, you will need to run multiple scenarios based on your anticipated expectations. These different scenarios will clearly illustrate the financial advantages of paying points or not paying points.

Somewhere in the future you will find a breakeven point where you will be out of the red and into the black; you'll have recovered the amount you paid in points through your lower payment. Based on this breakeven date, you can determine whether it would be prudent for you to pay points. It all comes down to that most important question:

How long are you going to carry this mortgage?

Make sure you're working with someone who understands the future break-even point when considering paying points on a mortgage loan, because it may not be in your best interest.

The Cost of Waiting to Sell

When most people consider selling their home, they think about one thing and one thing only — how much are they going to make from the sale?

Often, people delay selling their home when they think they won't profit because the housing market is down. Recently, the housing market has been down, and interest rates have been extremely low. It's important to understand that, when you sell a property, you may not be selling at the top of the market, but you're going to be buying a new property at a lower price than if you waited for prices to rise.

Other things to take into consideration are interest rates, the fluctuation of interest rates, and their effect on your monthly payment and your overall financial picture if you wait to sell. Interest rates were at historic lows at the end of 2012 and the beginning of 2013, but many people still waited to sell their home because they didn't think their house value was back to where it "should be."

With loan amounts above $150,000, an interest rate increase of 1% will typically result in a monthly payment

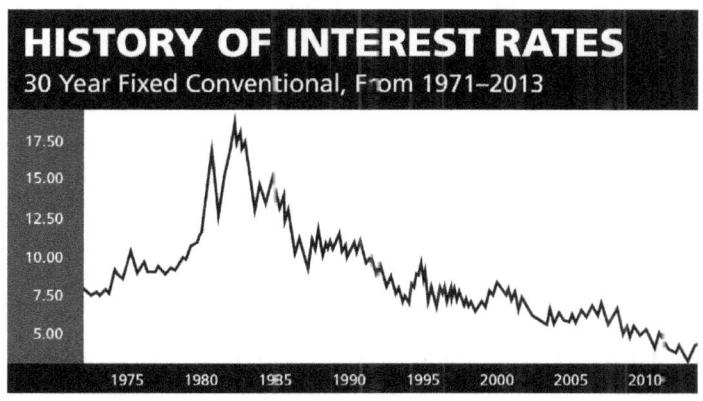

increase of at least $100. Those who didn't act missed taking advantage of these historically low interest rates, hoping to profit more from the sale of their home. They didn't consider the savings a lower interest rate would have generated and they missed the big picture by focusing on the small picture. Study the above graph and you can see why this is the case.

How to Sell Your House without Moving

Have you noticed that your house is worth much more than it was 10 years ago? You may worry that your home's value will soon fall; after all, in many parts of the country, the real estate market is not as strong as it was even five to ten years ago. If you are afraid that your home's value might fall, you should sell the house before that happens.

But say you don't want to do that because it's your home, after all. You have roots in the community, you don't want to uproot your kids, and where would you move? No, selling is not a good idea. Still, you are worried that your home's equity is at risk. How can you protect your home's equity without selling? The easiest way is to Sell Without Moving.

To Sell Without Moving means you simply get a new mortgage, or refinance, and pull the accumulated equity out of the house. It has the same effect as selling, except you don't have to sell… or move. Here's how it works:

The Mortgage Book

Say you bought a house for $200,000 with no money down (even though that's highly unlikely these days), meaning you initially owed $200,000 on your mortgage. Furthermore, say that the prices have skyrocketed in your neighborhood, and your house is now worth $500,000. You are concerned that the prices won't stay this high and will soon begin to drop. If you sell now for $500,000, assuming you can get back all the fees involved with selling, moving, etc., you'd pocket $300,000. But you don't want to sell, so you refinance instead, and get a new loan for $500,000. You now have that extra $300,000 in hand, just as if you'd sold the house.

Obviously, this is an extreme example, and I'm not suggesting you actually get a new mortgage that is two and a half times your current mortgage, although in some situations, this would be a good idea. Refinancing—or Selling Without Moving—provides access to the equity in your house now, as you can't do this after the value falls.

For example, if you plan to use the equity in your home to put the kids through college, you should get the loan now, so that you don't have to worry in the future about falling values wiping out your kids' college fund.

The Mortgage Book

I'm not suggesting that you'd want to owe more on the house than it's actually worth, but that's certainly better than watching the equity evaporate before you have a chance to use it. As long as you don't utilize this cash through lifestyle consumption, you are in a more secure financial position if the value of your home does drop.

Get the equity out of the house now, while you can. There are many people throughout America who wish they had done this back in the early 2000s. People in Florida, Arizona, Texas and California have watched the value of their homes plummet, and their equity disappear. Had they Sold Without Moving, they definitely would be in a better financial situation today.

When you Sell Without Moving, you can use the money for college, remodeling, vehicles, and even retirement income strategies. This type of thinking is yet another example of how you can use your mortgage to help expand your overall financial wealth.

Don't Let Your Mortgage Hold You Back

Eight months ago, I met with a dentist who had a 10-year mortgage, with a monthly payment around $3,000. The dentist was currently working for a well-established dental practice in the Little Rock area, but he wanted to get out on his own and start his own practice. He was afraid to take that step, though, because he had this $3,000-a-month house payment.

When he visited with me, we discussed his overall financial position and his future goals. After looking at a number of options, we moved him from a 10-year note to a 30-year note, freeing up $2,200 a month in cash flow. He then felt more comfortable about moving forward with opening his own dental practice, because his monthly cash outlay had been drastically reduced by the refinance.

Yes, we extended the term of the loan, and yes, the interest rate went up; but this allowed the dentist to achieve his dream of being his own boss. In the future, this refinance could save the dentist from losing his practice. By establishing a relationship with a mortgage professional who understands these concepts, your mortgage can be structured to help your reach your goals.

The Steps to Obtaining a Mortgage

There are many steps in the process of obtaining a mortgage loan. My desire here is to give you a high-level view so you can picture how the process should transpire.

The first step is to complete a mortgage application, which requires anywhere from 15 to 30 minutes. During the application, you'll be asked a series of questions to define what needs to be accomplished. During the application, your credit report is obtained. After the application is complete, you will need to provide some specific documentation to your lender. Those items usually consist of:

- Driver's License
- Social Security Card
- Pay Stubs
- W2s
- Tax Returns, and

The Mortgage Book

- Asset Statements

After your application has been completed and all required documentation has been provided to your lender, you need to have a mortgage planning consultation.

Then, typically within a day or two, your file will be submitted for underwriting approval through an automated system. After an underwriting system approves your loan, you will receive a pre-approval letter. This letter will allow you to make an offer on a property.

Once a real estate contract has been finalized between you and the seller, you should have your second mortgage planning session. During this mortgage planning session, you will walk through the final steps of the mortgage planning process. After deciding on the best loan structuring option for you, you'll typically lock in an interest rate. You will then need to sign a set of preliminary loan documents.

The lender then gets to work processing your mortgage. The lender will verify your financial information: employment, income, deposits, and so forth. The lender will also request title work and an appraisal on the home you're purchasing or refinancing. This is required to support the property's value or purchase price (remember: the value of a house is *not* determined by the mortgage, but by comparable homes in the area). A professional appraiser will contact the appropriate party to arrange for this to be performed.

Once the lender has received all the required documentation, your loan request is submitted to their (human) underwriter for approval. After reviewing the loan in full, the underwriter may request additional information. If this happens, you simply provide this information as soon as possible so your loan can be approved quickly.

When your loan is approved, you will be contacted to schedule a convenient time to close with the title company. Once your closing is scheduled, you will be required to obtain one years' worth of homeowners insurance on the property; the policy should be in place a couple of days prior to closing.

A day or two prior to closing, you will be notified of the amount you'll need to bring to the closing in the form of a cashier's check or money order (no personal checks, please).

The Mortgage Book

On the day of your closing you will need to bring your cashier's check made out in the correct amount, a copy of your driver's license and another form of ID. Closing typically takes 30 minutes to an hour, and at this time you will sign a stack of documents. IF you like (or desire) to read everything before you sign it, you should request the paperwork 2-3 days prior to closing so the closing is more efficient.

Once you leave the closing, the deed will be recorded, and the house will be yours.

Congratulations!

In Closing

As you have followed Dave and Sue on their journey of home ownership, you've learned about a number of factors that affect your mortgage decision and financial future. By understanding the 6-Step Mortgage Planning Process, you now know that searching for the lowest interest rate is not the optimum starting point.

Obtaining a mortgage is one of the largest financial transactions you will ever make. You should work with a mortgage professional who can give you wise counsel and who has a plan you can follow to help you achieve your short- and long-term financial goals.

Mortgage Industry Terms

Annual Percentage Rate (APR)

The APR takes into consideration the fees or costs associated with a loan, and expresses them to you as the cost of credit in relation to the amount borrowed. The lending institution shows you this mathematical calculation at the beginning of the mortgage application process on the Truth in Lending disclosure.

Adjustable-Rate Mortgage (ARM)

A mortgage with a clause permitting the interest rate to adjust periodically based on a standard financial index.

Amortization

The way interest and principal are paid off over the life of a loan. With home mortgages, early payments are comprised primarily of interest while the final payments are comprised almost entirely of principal.

Appraisal

A written report, by a qualified appraiser, estimating the value of a specific property. This report is based on the value of comparable properties.

Closing Costs

Expenses paid at the time of closing for third party items. They can include the costs of the transaction for obtaining a new loan, or paying for services performed, such as the appraisal, termite inspection, government fees, title fees, taxes and other such items.

Conventional Loan

Mortgage loans not insured by the federal government. Guidelines for these loans are set by Fannie Mae and Freddie Mac. They are typically more suitable for people with higher credit scores.

Credit Score

A number that expresses an individual's credit-worthiness.

Down Payment

The amount of a property's purchase price that the buyer pays in cash and does not finance.

Down Payment Assistance

Programs available to assist the purchaser with the cost of down payment. Arkansas has some down payment assistance programs; they are administered through the Arkansas Department of Financial Authority, (ADFA).

Equity

The difference between the value of a home (based on a current appraisal) and the balance owed on the mortgage and any other outstanding loans against the house.

Escrow Account

An escrow account holds funds for taxes and insurance. It increases with each monthly payment by the amount allocated for taxes and insurance. When annual tax and insurance bills come due, they are paid out of the escrow account. The amount allocated may vary annually with changes to tax rates, your home's appraised value and insurance premiums, thus changing the monthly mortgage payment.

FHA Loan

The loan program insured by the Federal Housing Administration (FHA). This loan program requires a minimum 3.5% down payment. FHA loans require an upfront mortgage insurance premium and an annual mortgage insurance premium, which is included in the monthly payment.

Fannie Mae

The Federal National Mortgage Association (FNMA), commonly known as Fannie Mae, is a government-sponsored enterprise (GSE) whose purpose is to expand the secondary mortgage market by securitizing mortgages in the form of mortgage-backed securities. This allows lenders to reinvest their assets into more lending and effectively increases the number of lenders in the mortgage market by reducing the reliance on locally based Savings and Loan associations (also known as "Thrifts").

Fixed Rate Mortgage

A mortgage where the interest rate stays the same (remains "fixed") throughout the life of the loan.

Freddie Mac

The Federal Home Loan Mortgage Corporation (FHLMC), known as Freddie Mac, is a public government-sponsored enterprise (GSE) created to expand the secondary market for mortgages in the US. Freddie Mac buys mortgages on the secondary market, pools them, and sells them to investors on the open market as mortgage-backed securities.

Good Faith Estimate (GFE)

A written estimate of expected closing costs provided by a lender to a prospective homebuyer. Regulations are in place to ensure lenders attempt to be as accurate as possible when providing these estimates.

Home Equity Indebtedness

When paying cash for a home, the buyer has 90 days to obtain financing on that house. Otherwise, interest on any loan against that house is <u>not</u> tax-deductible.

Home Inspection

The examination of a home, typically conducted by a trained professional, and normally completed in conjunction with the purchase of a new residence.

> **Note:** I always recommend getting a home inspection on a property before purchasing it.

Homeowner's Insurance

Insurance covering a residence in case of loss or damage. It is always paid in advance by a year. It should not be chosen strictly on a lowest cost basis.

> **Note:** I recommend getting quotes and comparing coverage from multiple companies when selecting your homeowner's insurance, and being sure to purchase and maintain "replacement cost" coverage. (This may change as the value of your home increases.)

Income Verification

A procedure completed by the mortgage lender. We have many different ways of verifying income: W2s, federal tax returns, pay stubs, 4506s from the IRS and verifications of employment from your employer are just a few.

Mortgage Insurance (PMI)

Private mortgage insurance purchased by the loan borrower to protect the lender from non-payment of the loan. It is typically required when obtaining a conventional loan and making a down payment of less than 20%.

PITI (Principal-Interest-Taxes-Insurance)

The components of mortgage payments. Mortgage insurance, if applicable, may also be included.

Points

Upfront fees paid to lower mortgage interest rates. These fees generate a lower interest rate, and consequently a lower monthly payment. Each "point" equals 1% of the total loan amount. For example, one point on a $200,000 loan equals $2,000.

Prepaids

Expenses that are "pre-paid" at closing. Typically consisting of real estate taxes, insurance and interest.

Pre-Qualified Buyer

A potential purchaser designated as worthy of obtaining a loan by a lender. Typically, the purchaser must complete a mortgage application and provide supporting documentation before a lender can reach this determination.

> **Note:** It is always helpful to get prequalified prior to searching for homes to ensure you know what you can afford and to determine the down payment and monthly payments associated with the homes you are considering. Prequalification is based on borrower income and ability to repay the loan, not on any money the borrower has in the bank or on the collateral (the house).

Rural Development Loan

A loan program administered through the government to help promote urban growth. This program does not require a down payment, but properties must be located in a specific geographical area to be eligible and the purchaser must incur an upfront funding fee and monthly mortgage insurance premium.

Seller Financing

A loan provided by the seller of a property to the purchaser.

Taxes (Real Estate)

Taxes homeowners are responsible for paying based on the assessed value of their home. Taxes are always paid in arrears; you pay taxes for the previous year every April when they come due.

Termite Contract

A contract between a homeowner and a company to protect the homeowner from the ramifications of termite damage.

Note: You should always keep a termite contract on your home if you live in a region where termites are active.

Title Insurance

A policy that guarantees the homeowner has proper title to a property and can legally transfer title to someone else. The title insurer pays for any damages if a discrepancy occurs. These policies protect the lender and the purchaser.

VA Loan

A loan guaranteed by the U.S. Department of Veterans Affairs (the VA). These loans were designed to offer financing options to eligible veterans or their surviving spouses. The VA loan does not require any down payment on the property being purchased but it does require an upfront "funding fee."

Author Biography

Lee Welfel is a seasoned mortgage-lending specialist. His unique approach and his 6-Step Mortgage Planning Process gives his clients the information they need to make the best overall financial decision.

Lee lives in Maumelle, Arkansas with his wife, Kelly, and sons Dylan and Hudson. He loves to be outdoors and enjoys grilling out, playing soccer and spending time with his family.

Lee understands that your mortgage is one of the largest financial decisions you will ever make and he takes the time to ensure you are not putting yourself or your family at risk.

Lee says, "My mission is to educate my clients so that they are able to integrate their mortgage into their overall financial goals."

You can contact Lee through his website: www.LeeWelfel.com.

www.ingramcontent.com/pod-product-compliance
Lightning Source LLC
Chambersburg PA
CBHW051710170526
45167CB00002B/613